JOURNEYS
TO SIGNIFICANCE

Ancient Philippi, where Paul first reached Europeans with the Gospel on his second journey.

JOURNEYS
TO SIGNIFICANCE

CHARTING A
LEADERSHIP COURSE
FROM THE LIFE OF PAUL

NEIL COLE

JOSSEY-BASS
A Wiley Imprint
www.josseybass.com

cation

Published by Jossey-Bass
A Wiley Imprint
989 Market Street, San Francisco, CA 94103-1741—www.josseybass.com

Jossey-Bass books and products are available through most bookstores. To contact Jossey-
Bass directly call our Customer Care Department within the U.S. at 800-956-7739,
outside the U.S. at 317-572-3986, or fax 317-572-4002.

Jossey-Bass also publishes its books in a variety of electronic formats. Some content
that appears in print may not be available in electronic books.

Library of Congress Cataloging-in-Publication Data

Cole, Neil, date
    Journeys to significance: charting a leadership course from the life of Paul / Neil Cole.
        p. cm.—(Jossey-Bass leadership network series; 48)
    Includes index.
    ISBN 978-0-470-52944-7 (hardback); 978-1-118-00543-9 (ebk);
    978-1-118-00544-6 (ebk); 978-1-118-00545-3 (ebk)
        1. Paul, the Apostle, Saint.   2. Christian leadership.   I. Title.
    BS2506.3.C64   2011
    225.9'2—dc22
                                                            2010046806

Printed in the United States of America
FIRST EDITION
HB Printing   10 9 8 7 6 5 4 3 2 1

— Leadership Network Titles —

Whole Church: Leading from Fragmentation to Engagement, Mel Lawrenz

Culture Shift: Transforming Your Church from the Inside Out, Robert Lewis and Wayne Cordeiro, with Warren Bird

Church Unique: How Missional Leaders Cast Vision, Capture Culture, and Create Movement, Will Mancini

A New Kind of Christian: A Tale of Two Friends on a Spiritual Journey, Brian D. McLaren

The Story We Find Ourselves In: Further Adventures of a New Kind of Christian, Brian D. McLaren

Missional Renaissance: Changing the Scorecard for the Church, Reggie McNeal

Practicing Greatness: 7 Disciplines of Extraordinary Spiritual Leaders, Reggie McNeal

The Present Future: Six Tough Questions for the Church, Reggie McNeal

A Work of Heart: Understanding How God Shapes Spiritual Leaders, Reggie McNeal

The Millennium Matrix: Reclaiming the Past, Reframing the Future of the Church, M. Rex Miller

Your Church in Rhythm: The Forgotten Dimensions of Seasons and Cycles, Bruce Miller

Shaped by God's Heart: The Passion and Practices of Missional Churches, Milfred Minatrea

The Missional Leader: Equipping Your Church to Reach a Changing World, Alan J. Roxburgh and Fred Romanuk

Missional Map-Making: Skills for Leading in Times of Transition, Alan J. Roxburgh

Relational Intelligence: How Leaders Can Expand Their Influence Through a New Way of Being Smart, Steve Saccone

Viral Churches: Helping Church Planters Become Movement Makers, Ed Stetzer and Warren Bird

The Externally Focused Quest: Becoming the Best Church for the Community, Eric Swanson and Rick Rusaw

The Ascent of a Leader: How Ordinary Relationships Develop Extraordinary Character and Influence, Bill Thrall, Bruce McNicol, and Ken McElrath

Beyond Megachurch Myths: What We Can Learn from America's Largest Churches, Scott Thumma and Dave Travis

The Other Eighty Percent: Turning Your Church's Spectators into Active Disciples, Scott Thumma and Warren Bird

The Elephant in the Boardroom: Speaking the Unspoken About Pastoral Transitions, Carolyn Weese and J. Russell Crabtree

Contents

To Dana, my love. As I pause and look back over the
course of all my own journeys, one thing stands out:
Dana, you are, without a doubt, the second best decision
of my life. I constantly thank the very best decision for giving
me the wisdom to say, "I do" on that June morning, and
for the greater miracle of persuading you to do the same.
There have been many times you have had to wait for me
to catch up on our journeys, but I am grateful for your
willingness to walk through them all with me.

About Leadership Network

Leadership Network's mission is to accelerate the impact of OneHundredX leaders. These high-capacity leaders are like the hundredfold crop that comes from seed planted in good soil as Jesus described in Matthew 13:8.

Leadership Network . . .

- explores the "what's next?" of what could be.
- creates "aha!" environments for collaborative discovery.
- works with exceptional "positive deviants."
- invests in the success of others through generous relationships.
- pursues big impact through measurable kingdom results.
- strives to model Jesus through all we do.

Believing that meaningful conversations and strategic connections can change the world, we seek to help leaders navigate the future by exploring new ideas and finding application for each unique context. Through collaborative meetings and processes, leaders map future possibilities and challenge one another to action that accelerates fruitfulness and effectiveness. Leadership Network shares the learnings and inspiration with others through our books, concept papers, research reports, e-newsletters, podcasts, videos, and online experiences. This in turn generates a ripple effect of new conversations and further influence.

In 1996 Leadership Network established a partnership with Jossey-Bass, a Wiley Imprint, to develop a series of creative books that provide thought leadership to innovators in church ministry. Leadership Network Publications present thoroughly researched and innovative concepts from leading thinkers, practitioners, and pioneering churches.

Leadership Network is a division of OneHundredX, a global ministry with initiatives around the world.

To learn more about Leadership Network, go to www.leadnet.org

To learn more about OneHundredX, go to www.100x.org

A well said to have belonged to Paul's family in Tarsus.

Preface and Acknowledgments

*In little more than ten years St. Paul established the church in
four provinces of the Empire: Galatia, Macedonia, Achaia, and
Asia. Before A.D. 47 there were no churches in these provinces;
in A.D. 57 St. Paul could speak as if his work there was done,
and could plan extensive tours into the far west without anxi-
ety lest the churches which he had founded might perish in his
absence for want of his guidance and support.*
—Roland Allen

*One thing I do: forgetting what lies behind and reaching
forward to what lies ahead, I press on toward the goal for the
prize of the upward call of God in Christ Jesus.*
—the apostle Paul (Philippians 3:13–14)

Finding My Way on a Road Without Signs

After finishing some meetings in Indiana, I had rushed to the Fort Wayne
airport only to find that my flight to Chicago had been canceled. In
Chicago I was supposed to conduct a seminar on leadership formation,
but the airline had canceled the forty-minute shuttle because of weather
conditions.

In Fort Wayne the night sky was beautifully clear, and it wasn't even
cold. Chicago was less then two hundred miles distant, so how could
there be that sort of extreme weather only a short jump away from such
a calm night sky?

I was angry. I suspected that airline officials were lying about why
they had canceled the flight. My nastier self was convinced that they just
didn't have enough passengers to warrant the expense of the flight and
had used the weather as an excuse to cancel it. I can be such a cynic!

I had no other option but to rent a car and launch into the four-hour drive. It was already close to eight o'clock in the evening, and my seminar started at nine the next morning.

The drive on the toll road from Fort Wayne to Chicago was easy and uneventful, confirming my suspicions all the way. Around midnight, as I was approaching the Chicago city limits, I was talking on the phone with my wife when it started to snow. I told my wife the snow was pretty but certainly not heavy enough for flights to be canceled. But as I drove on and entered the city, the snow was really filling the air, and the wind off Lake Michigan was blowing so hard that the snow, heavy now, was blowing horizontally rather than falling vertically. The temperature had dropped, too, and it was extremely cold. It was so cold, in fact, that the snow blowing in off the lake was sticking to all the road signs, which had frozen. I couldn't even tell where I was, or where I was going. I began to question my initial skepticism, and soon I had to repent of my earlier anger and cynicism. Because of my judgmental attitude, I had some business to do with the Lord!

Meanwhile, I was effectively snow blind. Imagine trying to find a specific address in a large, unfamiliar city without the aid of highway or street signs! Although I could talk on the phone from my car, this was still before GPS became a feature of rental cars, and so my clear written-out directions to my hotel might as well have been Grandma's recipe for chocolate peanut butter cookies. I was alone, seemingly the only traveler lost on this four-lane highway in this snow-covered world. I felt as if I were trapped in an episode of *The Twilight Zone*—but without the signpost up ahead to tell me so! The only other person I came across was the lonely and cold tollbooth attendant, who either could not or would not help me out. Apparently all he could do was grunt.

I pulled off the road and into a parking lot, just to think and pray—and scream as I hit the roof of the rental car. It was now after one in the morning, and I was not feeling good about calling anyone in town that late. Besides, how could I even tell anyone where I was?

I might not have had a human guide, but I did have access to God, who always knows the right path. After some lengthy complaints, I finally asked Him to help me figure this situation out.

And an idea came to me. I drove on and pulled into a twenty-four-hour convenience store and requested a map. What good was a map, you may wonder, if I still couldn't read the highway signs? But the first step in finding your way is to recognize where you are. It is significantly helpful to find out how lost you really are! So first I had the clerk show me on the map just where I was.

Next I located where on the map I was supposed to be. It is important to know what your destination is. Where is it you really want to be? That tired adage is still true—he who aims at nothing hits it.

Then I looked carefully at the map and actually counted the number of highway off-ramps and the number of streets before each of the turns I would have to make in order to get to my destination. I took note of significant landmarks that would confirm that I was heading in the right direction. It was a desperate but feasible plan that I was determined to make work unless and until God provided another important piece of the solution.

As I walked out to my car with this plan, I noticed that a limo driver was finishing pumping gas into his car. As ingenious and creative as my own plan was, my Father gave me a better one. I asked this veteran of the streets of Chicago if he would be willing to guide me to my hotel, figuring that since he knew the path, he didn't need the street signs. He agreed. I drove in the dark, without signs, following someone who had been down the path before—all along checking my progress with the landmarks I had memorized from the map. I had already spent four and a half hours driving through rural Indiana, and now it took me another two hours to find my destination in Chicago. Never had a Holiday Inn looked so inviting!

Road signs are something we see every day, and yet we all take them for granted until we don't have any. Life doesn't usually come with lit-up street signs telling you when and where to turn next and what landmark is ahead. That's why you need a good map of the landmarks you can expect—and, hopefully, an experienced guide.

Think of this book as a guide to the road, with landmarks you can follow. Think of the apostle Paul as a seasoned vet who has followed the path before you and can now show you the way to your finish. Like Paul, we are called to find our own place in the unfolding journeys of our lives and to decide that nothing less than finishing well will do. In this book, I hope to point out some of the more obvious landmarks and paths of leadership formation that can guide you toward a strong finish to your life.

I do not in any way want to imply that I have lived out all the journeys that are described in this book. I hope not—I am too young to die! But, in reality, the only people qualified to write with that kind of authority about finishing well have already left this planet, leaving the rest of us to venture some ideas. Like Paul, I can say that I am still pressing on toward the goal; and, like Paul, I do know what the goal is—to finish well and become more like Christ with each step of the journey. I am not Paul, but I have lived enough, watched enough, and read enough that I can put down these thoughts even if some of the final chapters are still only a pursuit for my own life.

What makes this book different from the many similar books already available is that it does not just analyze Paul's life historically and present missional insights and theological implications. This book offers strategic missional lessons that can help you be more fruitful; but, even more, it focuses on the leadership formation that Paul went through. He is not just an example to missionaries, theologians, and church planters. He is an example, first of all, of a follower of Christ who demonstrates for us the paths we all must take to finish well. We can all follow him as he follows Christ.

For every leader there will be seasons when clear direction is sadly lacking and normal ways of operating are no longer useful. Lost in snow blindness, what will you do? Giving up, making excuses, shifting blame, shouting expletives, continuing to press the accelerator in false hope while heading in the wrong direction—all these paths are ill advised. We need to be able to depend on God for creative solutions that get us to our longed-for destinations.

If you are in a holding pattern and seem unable to make any of the progress you once hoped for, here are some important steps I learned in a freak snowstorm; they can apply to your own journey in leadership formation:

1. Pause and take a breath.
2. Get your bearings.
3. Take an inventory of your progress (or lack thereof).
4. Determine how it is God wants you to finish, and ask God to lead you forward from wherever you are now, step by step.
5. Courageously follow His lead, no matter what it costs you.

Finishing well is not something that you do at the end of your life—it is what you determine to do every day of your life. You do not finish well accidentally. Determine now that you will finish well or die trying—which, in the end, is really what it means to finish well.

Acknowledgments

During the summer months of 1994, I read two incredible books. And while I was reading them, I was also reading the book of Acts in its entirety.

The first of those two books was *Missionary Methods: Saint Paul's or Ours,* first published in 1912 and written by the late Anglican missionary Roland Allen.[1] I am in his debt, and I tread with much humility and caution as I set out to add anything to a subject so well treated by a scholar of his caliber. His work is profound. I want to say that his book was ahead of its time, but its wisdom is timeless, and its application is universal. If missional work is in your heart, read Roland Allen's books; you will not be disappointed.

The second book was *The Making of a Leader,* by J. Robert Clinton.[2] Dr. Clinton has devoted his life and his career to discovering the paths and processes of leadership formation, and his discoveries form much of the framework of this book. Though I regret that I have never met Dr. Clinton or taken any of his classes, he has been my instructor through his writing, especially the book I read in 1994. I am indebted to him for the years of hard work he invested in studying more than a thousand Christian leaders who have finished well.[3] He is a pioneer cartographer who went before us, marking and measuring the landscape and identifying the landmarks. Eventually he sketched out the first drafts of the maps that would later become the standard that guides us all. Any of us can turn to the back of our Bible and find maps of Paul's journeys, but the road map of this book follows the lines carefully drawn out by this able scholar and cannot be found in any copy of the Bible.

Thus I stood on very tall and broad shoulders in order to write this book, and the catalytic insights from my readings during the summer of 1994 took root in my mind and wouldn't let me go. It was during this period that I discovered the simple framework for this book. But it could not be written until I had actually walked some of the well-worn paths that were laid before me. As a result, this book has been sixteen years in the making, years in which I have been studying even more books, observing people, poring over Acts and the Pauline epistles, and, most of all, encountering many of their truths at first hand. The number of books written about the apostle Paul is apparently endless, and I have benefited greatly from all the outstanding scholarship that preceded me.

I also owe a debt of thanks to Bob Logan, who helped me to first publish and refine these thoughts. Bob is a key person whom I encountered on my own journey, and my life took a detour I have never regretted. In many ways, as Barnabas did for Paul, Bob took me off the bench and put me in the game.

My senior editor at Jossey Bass, Sheryl Fullerton, has helped me with three books so far, but none has demanded more of her skill and devotion than this one. It is not lost on me how much work she contributed to this book, and I owe her a debt of gratitude as well.

I am grateful to Chris Grant, and to my dear friends at Leadership Network as well, for their valuable assistance in getting this project and several others to publication.

Also deserving of thanks are two of my friends, Dr. Traver Dougherty and Dr. Randall Smith, who scrutinized the manuscript and gave me lots of helpful corrections and pointers. I was helped as well by the comments of Dr. Ian Scott.

It was very unusual, and not a coincidence in the least, that in the three years before I wrote this book my ministry brought me to visit almost all the places where Paul traveled over his life. I want to thank those who walked with me over the very rocks that Paul himself traveled. You have been the Barnabas (Carol Davis), Silas (Dezi Baker and Wolf Simson), and Timothy (Heather and Erin Cole) of my own life, and I love you all.

I also wish to express thanks to the people at Forest Home Christian Conference Center for providing me a secluded place where I could get this project done. In 1978, as a young student at that very campground, I was walking alone in the dark along a different kind of "road to Damascus." Snow was crunching under the weight of my every step. I was without a flashlight to guide me but could see the path well enough. Looking up through the dark silhouettes of tall pine trees, and beyond them, I saw an endless sky lit up by a canopy of unending stars. Occasionally a falling star whisked by, as if Heaven were winking at me. For the first time, I heard God's voice call out to me from the heavens above. I understood that there is a God to whom I will be accountable for my life, that He loves me, and that He came to us as the Son of Man—Jesus. And a year later, I surrendered to His call. It seems fitting that thirty years later I was drawn back to the place where my spiritual journey began, and where I could reflect on how it is that God leads us all on such journeys.

Laodicea, where a church was started during Paul's third journey by Epaphras.

Life Is a Series of Adventurous Journeys

Remember those who led you, who spoke the word of God to you; and considering the result of their conduct, imitate their faith. Jesus Christ is the same yesterday and today and forever.
—Hebrews 13:7–8

Be imitators of me, just as I also am of Christ.
—the apostle Paul (1 Corinthians 11:1)

My brother and I were born less than a year apart, and when were were in middle school we went on a safari to East Africa with our mother. This was an adventure most young boys only dream about. Anything but tame, the trip featured close encounters with wild animals of every kind.

Our journey took us first to a hotel on stilts, called Treetops, overlooking a water hole. Wild animals would come from miles around to drink at the water hole, and tourists like us could observe them from above in their natural habitat. Of course we were not the first ones to have had this view—the monkeys and baboons had been living in the treetops since long before tourists had ever stayed in that hotel. The afternoon when we checked in, we were warned to keep our windows closed so that these curious forest dwellers didn't steal our possessions while we were asleep. The primates were so at home at the Treetops that they would actually mingle with the guests, sometimes reaching right into their bags to take shiny objects such as cameras or glasses. I learned, however, not to think that these animals were tame simply because they were comfortable being close to people.

The morning after we arrived, I was on the top platform and saw a gray baboon reach into a woman's purse to steal her camera. He was close enough for me to reach out and touch him, and I was foolish enough to do it. I actually grabbed his tail, just for an instant, and in a flash the animal spun around, screaming with his mouth wide open. I saw teeth that were longer than my second-period math class and sharper than my classmate Rachel Cohen (who always skewed the grading curve higher). I quickly let go of the baboon's tail and froze with fear. The baboon took the camera and left. I'm surprised he didn't take a picture of the dumb look on my face, to give the rest of his troop a good laugh.

From Treetops, we traveled to the Amboselli game reserve. Our tour guide, hearing about my close encounter of the primate kind, decided to play a joke on me. He told me that the rhesus monkeys at our next stop were friendly toward tourists. When I found a monkey and tried to approach, it shrieked at me. I stepped back, and, seeing my timidity, the monkey stepped forward with new courage. Before I knew it, monkeys were dropping out of the sky to surround me, all of them screaming. Apparently they had all been in the tree over my head, and my trepidation had made them more brazen, too. And I, chased by a local gang of simian hoodlums defending their territory, took off running for my life. That evening I was not very hungry, so I decided to stay in our bungalow while my mother and my brother went up to the lodge for dinner. About dessert time, I had a remarkable recovery and felt hungry, so I decided to walk up to the lodge from our bungalow after dark. On the way to the lodge, I noticed something unusual, but since everything I was seeing was unusual to me, I didn't think much of it. Throughout the evening, there was usually one or another zebra or impala grazing on the lawn, but this time there were none to be found. The lights inside the dining area were glowing, and I could see all the people inside, but none were at their tables. They were all pressed up against the glass. looking—at me! They were also waving at me. Some seemed to be urging me to return to my bungalow, and others appeared to want me to hurry up and get inside. I had no clue why, but I sped up. Once inside, I was told that a leopard was out on the grass and had been stalking me. Fortunately, the sharpshooters had their rifles trained on her in case she wanted a little dessert herself. I remember wondering how many kids at my school could boast that a leopard had stalked them during summer vacation.

Within a couple of weeks, I had seen cheetahs, lions, giraffes, elephants, and hordes of wildebeest. I had ridden in a Land Rover chased by a rhinoceros, and I had been grunted at in a very threatening way by a bull. I had tried to catch foot-long lizards that lived in a palace (Proverbs

30:28) and had been bitten by more flies than Steven King could use in a horror movie.

At our last stop, I watched my brother feed a large multicolored bird, which looked as if it had a mohawk haircut made of feathers. The bird was a crested crane, and it lived in the hotel lobby, where tourists could buy seeds for a few coins and feed it. I figured I could handle this, but by now my reputation had spread throughout the animal kingdom. As I approached that beautiful bird, it squawked at me in a threatening way and advanced with its long neck and sharp beak. Startled, I stepped back, and it came after me. My mother watched me being chased through the lobby by a large brightly colored bird with long legs and a long neck.

I tell you this lengthy story of my journey in Africa because it has a lesson about life and significance. My brother and I were about the same age and of the same upbringing. But whereas I came home from that trip lucky to have all my fingers and lots of stories, my brother had spent most of the trip reading a novel about adventures in Africa! We both had a great time, but only one of us came home with stories to tell (and, obviously, I still do). There are two kinds of people in the world—those who live the adventure, and those who read about others' adventures. I determined a long time ago that I wasn't going to be someone who only read about the adventures of others. I would live the kind of life others would want to read about. I want a life of full-gusto, go-for-it faith that risks everything on the belief that God is indeed real and will carry me through. I want to live a life of increasing significance or die trying.

On Leadership

I believe that we need leaders who will live adventurous lives and grow in significance with each new journey. Simply put, we really need people willing to surrender everything for Jesus, every day. That's it. People who are willing to take a risk because Jesus first gave everything for them are the raw material that God can fashion into world changers. Leadership doesn't start with an education, an obvious spiritual gift, or a charming and electric personality. The journey to significance starts with the mere willingness to surrender the status quo and take the first step of faith into the adventure. That same willingness will take you each step of the way forward; it is the most important foundation of a leader's formation.

There are many books available on leadership today. A search for the word *leader* on the Amazon site returns almost 650,000 results, and the number seems to increase daily. One more published thought on the subject seems almost ridiculous. I myself have written three earlier resources addressing this subject.[1] Is leadership really that hard?

In its basic essence, leadership is not hard to define. In fact, you can literally sum it up in one word: *influence*. It is not hard to find books about good leadership, but finding someone who leads well is not as easy.

Many have defined leadership as getting other people to do what you want them to. That is influence, so I guess it is a form of leadership, albeit one that is selfish and manipulative. Even when we convince ourselves that we are really only doing what we know to be for the good of those we are manipulating, it is still an insult at best and deceptive at worst. It tends to treat everyone as a child incapable of making a good decision. It also leaves the people being influenced unprepared to eventually grow on their own and lead others.

The best leaders are not those who have the most followers but those who develop and deploy other leaders. The true test of a leader's influence is to look at what is left behind once the leader is gone. This lesson, however, is not something that one learns in an introductory course on leadership. It comes with the maturity that develops over the course of many struggles, setbacks and seeming failures. Perhaps this is why so few leaders today actually empower and release others but rather corral them in ministry contexts with the promise of services and entertaining productions. I wonder if our leaders have not fought through the lessons necessary to their becoming leaders who finish well and, as a result, have ended up simply casting their own vision and peddling their own influence. Instead of new leaders, the product of such influence peddlers is a growing congregation of consumers who beg to know "What have you done for me lately?" Or, as my friend Bob Logan says, "They're all tuned in to the same radio station—W-I-I FM, What's In It For Me?"

Why Another Book on Paul and Leadership?

What makes this book stand out from the 650,000 other books already available on leadership? There are many resources designed to teach you how to get others to help you get done what you want to accomplish. This is not that kind of book. There are also many books about how to develop other leaders. Some of those books say that leaders are made, and some of them say that leaders are born. This is not either kind of book. If anything, this book demonstrates that leadership is a both/and proposition. All are *born* to be *made* into influencers, whether that means bringing the Gospel to unreached groups of people, as Paul did, or raising children to be positive contributors to our society.

Another genre of leadership material looks at the kinds of character qualities necessary to being a good leader. Again, this book is not that sort of book. There are shelves of books that summarize the types of personalities and skills found in successful leaders. This book is not one of those. Some books look at the strategies and methods deployed by successful leaders, and this book is not strictly one of those, either, although there is some of that in here. There are also a lot of leadership biographies. But there are very few books that consider how God forms a leader over the course of a lifetime. This book is something of a blend of the last two kinds of book. I guess what makes this book unique is the way it treats its protagonist, the apostle Paul, and shows how his path to significance was actually quite a normal one that is available to us all.

The real trick is to be a successful leader in a context of difficult challenges. It is rare to lead throughout one's lifetime and to increase in significance all along so that one finishes strong and leaves a legacy of strong leaders to carry on the work. This book aims to discover how God forms that type of leader. And it would be very difficult to find a better example of a world-changing leader who finished strong than the apostle Paul.

From two thousand years ago, Paul calls to us: "Follow me as I follow Christ." This book takes that charge to heart, and it shows that you, too, can have increasing significance in life as you continue to follow the path toward Christ that Paul first laid down with his own steps. In this book we will examine the leadership trajectory of the apostle Paul and discover the ways he developed to become a man whom God used to change the world forever.

Some think that the church has emphasized Paul at the expense of Jesus. There may be truth in this accusation. I can understand why the church through the ages has been so enamored with Paul; he is, in a real sense, the father of the Gentile church. Two thousand years after his lifetime, he is still the apostle to the Gentiles. Whereas Jesus mentions the word *church* only twice, Paul clearly articulates what the church is to be about. When all is stripped away, however, the church is to be about Jesus. The church is focused on Paul, but he would say, "I have determined to know this: Jesus Christ and Him crucified." He always pointed us back to the true author and finisher of our faith—Jesus.

And so I believe that in order to understand Paul, one must first understand and love his Messiah, Jesus. My previous books, *Organic Church* and *Organic Leadership*, focus primarily on Jesus and His teachings that concern His kingdom.[2] It is with that foundation that I am now going to dive into the book of Acts and the epistles of Paul to discover what it takes to make a leader who can turn the world upside down and withstand the onslaught of evil to finish strong. In a sense, this book follows my previous publications, fleshing them out in order to describe what following Christ can look like in a life that is willing to surrender everything for the Lord.

Some scholars have taken to studying Paul's practices and compiling strategies built on his techniques. Several of these resources are exceptional and have had a great deal to do with my own understanding. Eckhard Schnabel's *Paul the Missionary: Realities, Strategies and Methods* and his two-volume *Early Christian Mission* are valuable recent additions to the library on Paul's strategies and the early church's expansion. F. F. Bruce's commentary on Acts and his *Paul: Apostle of the Heart Set Free* are outstanding and still set the bar for all subsequent works. The biographer John Pollock, in *The Apostle: A Life of Paul,* has done an outstanding job of synthesizing data from the New Testament as well as from geography, topography, and historical, cultural, and archaeological evidence. His narrative of Paul's life is both compelling and insightful. I highly recommend this book as well as all these other resources.[3]

On Paul the Learner

I have made it a personal life pursuit to understand the explosive expansion of Christ followers described in the book of Acts. In reading the book at least a hundred times over the past twenty years, I have discovered some aspects of Paul's developing leadership that I have not found in other books that cover his life. Most address Paul as a teacher of others, which of course he is. But I have come to see that the reason he is such a good teacher is that he is first a good learner.

In showing the lessons that Paul himself had to learn in order to become a better leader, this book seeks to show how we can all become better learners. Most books on Paul's missional strategies tend to summarize a strategy based on a comprehensive look at all he did, but this book observes how Paul adapted, and how he grew more effective with each journey. In some cases, Paul abandoned some strategies as he matured and embraced others that were more effective. To take all that he did and boil it down to a single strategy is almost an insult to Paul the learner and to his Lord the Teacher.

I fear that many of us have viewed the historical passages of Scripture concerning leaders like Paul (and Peter or Mary, if you are Catholic) through lenses that do not allow for such heroes to make mistakes. We view their practices with an almost superstitious regard for their infallibility. I do not believe that the apostle himself would want this sort of blind devotion. In fact, it is not fair to him. When we adulate him in this way, we steal his humanity from him, and he loses one of his most important qualities—his ability to adapt, learn, and mature. And if we forfeit those aspects of Paul, he ceases to be an example for us to follow.

When it comes to examining the lives of heroic leaders in the Bible, we have two choices: we can view these characters as exceptional, one-of-a-kind people or we can see them as ordinary people with an exceptional Savior. I suppose that the former option is preferable to those who wish to excuse their own lack of significance, but I always choose the latter. I truly believe that the stories found between the table of contents and the concordance of the Bible are there to inspire us to live better lives. If the people in those stories are too far removed from our ordinary lives, we will never even try to follow their examples. So I have sought to understand the humanity and frailty of Paul and tried to avoid making him out to be a superhero of unattainable skills and character.

We can all learn the same lessons that Paul did and grow in our own significance as leaders. In the end, none of us will be Paul. Hopefully, we will be the people Jesus desires us to be, just as Paul was the person Jesus desired him to be, and we will be people of expanding significance. We can all walk through journeys of increasing significance in whatever field God leads us into. What we will find is that Paul's formation as a leader was not at all exceptional, although the speed of his maturation and the intensity of his lessons are indeed exceptional and, as a result, his influence is unparalleled. Nevertheless, Paul's paths and processes are quite familiar to all leaders.

I've never been a great mathematician, but I learned a couple of profound equations a few years back. (Don't worry, they're not complicated.) The first is $0 + 0 = 0$. (Nothing remarkable there—pardon the pun.) The first equation becomes more revealing when it's followed by the second: $0 + \infty = \infty$. It is not the zero in the second equation that amounts to much. It is the ∞—the infinite—that matters. Only when the infinite is added to the zero does the sum become significant—in fact, immeasurable. Left to ourselves, we all amount to zero. This is true even for Paul, and he says as much (Philippians 3:7–8).

In the thirteenth chapter of the book of Hebrews, we are challenged to consider the lives of the leaders who have walked before us and to imitate their faith. It is in this context that the author writes the following words, which, unfortunately, we so often hear in a different context: "Jesus Christ is the same yesterday and today and forever." The word *forever* means "infinite." It is not the people whose stories are told in the Old Testament who are so exceptional. It is Jesus, the Infinite One, working through them Who causes the sum of their lives to be remarkable and worthy of storytelling. In all the eons of time, Jesus has not changed. The world is in as dire a state as ever. All that is needed in this equation is a willing zero to become the next hero. That is what Paul was—a zero willing to join with the infinite. Are you willing?

The Journeys of Life

It is common for people to view life as a journey, and in many ways it is. I am coming to see, however, that life is not just a single journey but is made up of several journeys, each full of new territory, exciting adventures, and life lessons to be learned. In this book, I break down how life's journeys build toward greater meaning and significance if one chooses to continue pressing forward.

Pressing forward means not remaining stuck in a single journey that continues to loop through the same lessons over and over again, unlearned each time. Leaders stuck in such a pattern will encounter all the different names and faces that come along, but they will have to learn the same remedial lesson over and over with increasing ferocity until they finally accept the lesson God intended. We simply cannot advance in our significance without learning what God is teaching us about us.

From his study of more than a thousand Christian leaders over the course of his career, J. Robert Clinton has identified six possible phases of growth that God takes a person through to develop a leader over the course of a lifetime. In this book, I have applied that formation process to the apostle Paul. The time line shows Clinton's stages lined up with Paul's Journeys.

Of course, as we all know, life does not follow neatly prescribed stages, with special graduation ceremonies at the end of each one to mark our passage forward and send us on our way. It would be nice, but I do not advise waiting for such. These phases of development are generalized and can even cross over into one another. There can also be boundaries between phases, and these boundaries can encompass periods when life feels stagnant and lacking in progress. These developmental stages are best viewed in hindsight, but they must be lived in blind forward progression. Not all the stages are guaranteed for all of us; in fact, few ever experience them all.

When I teach these things, people commonly try right away to find their own places in life's progressive journeys. Many of us tend to overestimate our progress to date, so I usually say, "When you think you have found your place, move at least one phase back and start there." If this

Time Line of Leadership Formation

	Phase I	Phase II	Phase III	Phase IV	Phase V	Phase VI
Clinton Stage	Sovereign foundations	Inner-life growth	Ministry maturation	Life maturation		
Journey of Paul	Birth and early life	Conversion and new life	First journey	Second journey	Third journey	Fourth journey and beyond
New Testament Passage	Philippians 3:5–6	Acts 7–13:3 Galatians 1:11–24	Acts 13–15 Galatians 2:1–10	Acts 16–18:22	Acts 18:23–20	Acts 21–28 1, 2 Timothy and Titus

sounds discouraging, I like to remind people of a few things. First, you do not become more spiritual as you progress, but simply more mature. Second, the journeys spelled out in this book are by no means a guarantee for everyone (in fact, few will ever experience the fourth journey mentioned in this book). And, third, it may be to your advantage that you are not as far along on these journeys as you are inclined at first to believe—it just may mean that you have longer to live. Don't be too anxious to rush life's development to the end.

This Book's Approach

Each of the chapters that follow begins by examining a phase of development in Paul's leadership. The second part of each chapter uses the lessons he learned during that phase to explore how all leaders go through similar developmental phases. We will discover how God molds a leader at each stage of formation. It is important for me to state that not all the descriptions of an emerging leader mentioned at each phase are true of Paul (nor are they relevant, for that matter, to all leaders). Some of the qualities I mention are not found in Paul's life, but they are common nevertheless. These are not strict formulas but general observations. Where there are connections with Paul's own development, I do my best to point them out. You may find that some of the descriptions are true of your own passage and some are not, and that's normal. Each of us is unique and has our own journey to follow, but there are some common characteristics that we can all learn from.

This book strikes a delicate balance, examining not only Paul's life and character development but also his strategy and methodology while relating his lessons to the lessons we all must learn. The book is not a commentary on Acts, nor is it, strictly speaking, a biography of Paul's life. My intention is not to force my paradigm for leadership formation on Acts but rather to draw out the parallels from Acts, and from the epistles, that help illustrate the patterns. Although I do not believe that Luke's intention in writing Acts was to teach these principles, we can still discover in Luke's story many common characteristics of a leader's maturation process. I have tried to keep this balance throughout the book, and I hope I have succeeded, but it is entirely possible that my observations are less than accurate, or that they are offered in a voice that is too certain. I am capable of mistakes, but this is a resource for learning, and all good learning requires risk.

There are some unavoidable gaps in Acts that I have tried to fill in a way that makes sense, on the basis of my having studied many excellent resources devoted to answering questions about Paul's life. But in the end, I had to make my own choices about chronology, geography, and motivations. For the most part, I have not explained those choices, but if I felt that some explanation was warranted, I included my reasoning in the notes. Whenever I have moved from clearly recorded history into speculation, I have tried my best to speak in a voice that will allow for other options, although I have not always expounded on all the options. This book is not a composite history but a study of the leadership formation of a foundational character of history.

Although this book was written in a fairly narrative style, I intend it to be a missionally strategic resource, not a dissection of Acts. In unfolding the story, I often have not cited scriptural references for all the narration, since that would only serve to interrupt the flow. You can simply follow along in Acts if you want specific "addresses" for the various parts of the story. Nevertheless, I have included references for insights gleaned from other passages in Acts that shed light on where we are in the story.

If we are to return to a missional expression of ecclesia, we simply must take a fresh look at the book of Acts as well as at Paul's life and letters, and we must evaluate our own experience in their light. We may also find that approaching the New Testament with a fresh perspective sheds new light on the truth found there as well. This is not to force our own bias or culture on the New Testament but actually to remove lenses that were once forced upon us, lenses that have caused us to place the Scriptures into an old and culturally biased container that is not necessarily suitable.

We will discover some of the profound strategic lessons that Paul learned and adopted so that he could be more productive and influential with different groups, finish strong, and develop as a leader. All those lessons are important to a missional approach. I have not taken anything away from the great apostle, but at the same time I have tried to demonstrate how normal his pattern of development is, and how we all must journey along similar paths.

None of us can claim yet to have the type of success that Paul has had. But all of us can aspire to go further on the journeys that expand our significance. Not everyone is an apostle, and we all have different callings to pursue, but we are all intended to grow and mature in Christlikeness and thus to have greater influence on those around us. In this very important way, we can all learn from the life of Paul. Perhaps in the days ahead, new Pauls and Paulines will arise and change our world forever. Be a willing zero, and you, too, can have a story that others will tell.

JOURNEYS
TO SIGNIFICANCE

BEGINNINGS

PART ONE

The monastery at Petra where Paul likely visited during his time in Arabia.

The Wailing Wall in Jerusalem.

1

Born to a Destiny

The Fingerprints of God
on the Early Years

Everything is determined, the beginning as well as the end,
by forces over which we have no control. It is determined for
the insect as well as for the star. Human beings, vegetables,
or cosmic dust, we all dance to a mysterious tune, intoned in
the distance by an invisible piper.
—Albert Einstein

God had set me apart even from my mother's womb.
—the apostle Paul in his letter to the Galatians (Galatians 1:15)

FROM A HUMAN POINT OF VIEW, there is nothing remarkable about Paul's birth and early life that we are aware of. There is no indication that this was a man who would forever leave his mark on history. His parents did not have angelic visitations. New stars did not appear overhead to guide people to his crib. There were no shepherds hearing angelic choirs or Magi bearing gifts from the east to his humble home.

But the hand of a Sovereign God left fingerprints all over Paul's early life. He was born to a destiny. Later in life, he understood this and commented that God had set him apart even from the time of his conception. He would find that the Lord had been preparing him all his life for his calling, and for the journeys that were planned for him. If you have the right lenses, you may also see that you were born to a destiny (Ephesians 2:6–10). The evidence may be all around you, waiting to be discovered.

Paul's Birth and Early Life

Paul was born to a devout Jewish family in the city of Tarsus, in what is now Turkey, where he spent his formative years during the Pax Romana, the peace of Rome. It wasn't that those days were particularly peaceful for the people, but the Empire had sufficiently beaten down all other competitors for power to stand alone as the ruling government of the world. The Roman Empire during this time expanded its influence by building up its cities and increasing its roadways and shipping. As a result, the known world became smaller in many ways.

Paul was born in a time ripe for the work he would be chosen to do. The Roman roads laid out a path for him and his team that connected all the important trade routes. There was a common and prevalent trade language—Koine Greek—in which Paul could communicate with people from other lands even when he didn't know their native tongues or have a translator available. The shipping routes were established, with many ships from around the empire constantly arriving at and leaving from almost every port. Jewish synagogues and communities, established in most cities, presented him with a ready-made beachhead for almost all of his missionary endeavors.

In his Jewish family, which could trace its history to the tribe of Benjamin (Philippians 3:4–6), Paul was steeped in the Torah from his earliest days (Deuteronomy 6:1–10). This lineage was very important to his parents, for they raised their son to be a highly committed man of faith, fluent in Mosaic law and knowledgeable about the prophets of the Old Testament. It is unlikely that they were Jewish in name only or mere cultural Israelites; more probably they were very committed to their heritage. Paul said of his upbringing that he had been "circumcised the eighth day, of the nation of Israel, of the tribe of Benjamin." He referred to himself as a "Hebrew of Hebrews" and "as to the Law, a Pharisee" (Philippians 3:4–6).[1]

His parents gave him the name of the most famous historical leader of the tribe of Benjamin, the first king of Israel, Saul. Paul mentions his namesake only once, in a sermon in Psidian Antioch on his first journey, when he says that God gave the Israelites Saul when they asked for a king. He says that Saul was the son of Kish and from the tribe of Benjamin (which to Paul may have been the only good thing he could say about this character, and the only thing the two seemed to have in common) and that he ruled for forty years, until God removed him and replaced him with a king who followed His own heart—David (Acts 13:21–22). Unlike Saul, Paul would be the epitome of one sold out for a cause greater than himself, first for the defense of Israel but ultimately for the person of Jesus.

Paul's family was probably committed to the Pharisaical expression of Judaism, which means that they would have placed great emphasis on observing both Mosaic law and probably oral Torah as well, much later to be written down and called the Talmud. He would have been trained from his earliest days to view life through these lenses and to see the world as clean or unclean, pure or impure, good or bad. This sectarian mind-set developed into an all-or-nothing personality, which exhibits itself throughout Paul's life, whether he is hunting down Christians to arrest them or himself standing trial before the emperor for his own faith in Jesus Christ.

Most scholars assume that because Paul held *civis Romanus,* Roman citizenship, he came from a fairly wealthy family. As Acts 22:28 tells us, Roman citizenship was expensive, and it was passed along to him by virtue of his birth. Even if his family had been given Roman citizenship earlier, for heroic service to the emperor (which is also a possibility), it nevertheless provided Paul's family with opportunities that could elevate their status and their standard of living. It was also very valuable to Paul later on, when he began his travels among the first Christians. As a Roman citizen, he could not be punished without a fair trial, and any arrests had to follow a certain protocol, which required that he be treated with greater respect. In actuality, his citizenship seems never to have prevented his arrest, but it did make the arrests more tolerable at times and even gave him, finally, the opportunity to go to Rome to stand before Caesar. He used this privilege a few times over the course of his journeys (Acts 16:37; 22:25; 25:16).

Unlike many Christian leaders today, who are devoted to ministry, all good Pharisaic scholars and teachers had to earn their livelihoods by acquiring and practicing a trade. It is likely that Paul learned his trade as a tent maker from his father, as was customary in those days.[2] Whenever the need arose, he could make a living plying his trade, a useful one in every part of the empire.

Having grown up in a Roman city and then gone to study in Jerusalem, Paul learned several languages. He spoke Greek fluently and could perhaps read and understand some Latin as well. Tarsus was the leading city of Cilicia, which was under the province of Syria during Paul's lifetime, and so he may have also understood some of the indigenous Cilician dialect, although this is not at all certain. Because of his parents' religious devotion, he may have spoken Aramaic at home, although Greek often became the native language among the diaspora. Given his strict training in Jerusalem, he would also have learned Hebrew (Acts 22:2; Philippians 3:5). God's sovereign hand is evident, for Paul would later demonstrate an aptitude for learning languages and would write eloquently in the Koine Greek, the lingua franca of his day.[3]

Some make much of the fact that Tarsus, a city that would have been a thousand years old by the time of Paul's birth, was a center for culture, with schools that were devoted to philosophy, rhetoric, and law. I believe that this would have had great influence on Paul, but not so much during his youth, when I believe he would have been somewhat protected from such influence by his devout Jewish home. No doubt the influence of the culture around him helped to prepare him for his call to the Gentiles after his conversion.

In some ways, Paul was what we today would call a "third culture" kid—not only Jewish and not only Roman but also of a third culture made up of both. Granted, his family would have been committed to life in a separate Jewish subculture, but he was still immersed in a leading Roman city and was affected by that experience. If he had been born and raised only in Israel, he could easily have known only Jewish culture, which would have made him less able to adapt to and learn other cultures and languages. But because he was born and lived in Tarsus, he had many advantages for the work he would ultimately set out to accomplish. He could be at home everywhere he went and yet not feel the need to stay, because he never truly fit in anywhere.

As a Jew growing up far from Jerusalem, he probably came to see that his religious beliefs were not bound by geography. Once he came to see Jesus as the Way, all that he had once learned from the Torah and about Jewish law and teaching began to take on far greater significance. In a sense, he was being educated into his destiny even before he could possibly have understood its significance.

It is possible that his family made the pilgrimage to Jerusalem on rare occasions for religious holy days.[4] Such travels may have begun the pattern that would govern all of Paul's life—taking journeys for his belief in God.

It has been commonly assumed that at some point Saul of Tarsus was married and had at least one child. That was required of members of the Sanhedrin, a high court of Israel made up of seventy-one members who met daily in the temple to govern the Jewish affairs of the day, although there is not really any evidence that Saul was a member of the Sanhedrin.[5] Regardless, a good Pharisee always married and had a family; that was the expectation for such a role.

But if he did have a family, it is not known what became of his wife and child, since neither Paul nor Luke mentions either. There is much room for speculation and none for factual assertion. Perhaps both died at some point, causing Paul to seek solace in greater devotion to his work. Could it be that his pain was reflected in the passion with which he persecuted the Christians? We cannot know, but Paul decided to remain single when he became a Christian. He even seems to imply that he had a gift for remaining celibate (1 Corinthians 7:7–8). Paul said, "Are you bound to a wife? Do not seek to be released. Are you released from a wife? Do not seek a wife" (1 Corinthians 7:27). He concedes that it would not be wrong to marry, but that one who does loses some of the focus on mission that comes with not being bound in marriage (1 Corinthians 7:32–35). He also mentions that other apostles had the right to take their wives with them on their journeys, but that he and Barnabas chose not to (1 Corinthians 9:5–6). We can conclude from these passages that he was single at the time of his conversion and remained single, and that leaves us to speculate on what happened to his family, if indeed he ever had one. It does appear, however, when he writes to Christians about love, marriage, and parenting, that he has some experience to draw on.

Paul's Mentors

At some point in his young life (Acts 22:3; 26:4), Paul moved to Jerusalem and was trained to be a Pharisee. His enthusiasm must have been evident because the great Gamaliel, a respected Pharisee and teacher of Jewish law, chose to mentor him. Gamaliel's exceptional wisdom and respected status among his peers is demonstrated in that passage in the book of Acts where he advises the Sanhedrin, in the church's early days, not to execute the Apostles (Acts 5:33–42). He warns them that if the apostles' message is only of human origin, it will die all on its own, but if it is of God, it will not be stopped. Resisting it, he tells them, may even be fighting against God himself. Paul later mentions his teacher's name to gain some respect in a very tenuous situation (Acts 22:3). Later, as we shall see, Barnabas also became a mentor to Paul.

One of the needs of a leader who finishes well is to have mentors and to mentor others. Paul was blessed to have good mentors, and he would grow to become one himself.

The Mystery and Majesty of Destiny

In the movie *The Matrix*, Neo enters a dilapidated room in an abandoned building on a stormy night and is introduced to Morpheus, a legend he has only heard of. Morpheus is tall and dark, and he is wearing a long leather coat and reflective sunglasses. He is friendly and charming and walks with a bearing and confidence that imply a deeper knowledge of what life is all about.

Morpheus asks Neo whether he believes in fate. When Neo says he does not, Morpheus asks him why not. Neo tells him that he doesn't believe in fate because he doesn't like the idea that he is not in control of his life. Thus begins a conversation that ends with the revelation that all of Neo's life up to this moment has been a lie. Neo will soon come to realize that he has never had control of his life. But an awakening is about to occur that will not only grant Neo the truth but also eventually give him the freedom to choose the path of his life.

Neo, who comes to be the hero in the *Matrix* trilogy, discovers that he has a fate, a destiny for his own life, that was determined long ago. By stepping into that destiny, and believing in it, he will be able to set many captives free.

It is hard to believe in destiny. Surrendering to the idea that there is a master design for your life, one that you are meant to step into, is a pill that is hard to swallow. It doesn't matter whether you came from a charmed *Leave it to Beaver* childhood or from one full of deep scars and bitter memories; destiny is still a challenge. The idea of a personal fate threatens the hopeful future that some people carry with them every day—a fated life may end up being very different from the life someone desires. For others, the thought that their destiny is foreordained is troubling because it means that a personal God may have actually arranged for them to be born into a painful life. For still others, it may be troubling that their lives, dull or painful as they are, were destined for them. Some, like Neo, just want to maintain a sense of control over their lives. But whether we choose to accept the idea of destiny or not has no real bearing on its veracity. God has a unique calling for your life (Ephesians 2:10).

It is not the scope or theme of this book to address the eternal question of how our own free will works within the sovereignty of God, so I will not even attempt it. I will leave that to smarter men and other books. But when I say that you have a destiny, I mean that I believe God has advance knowledge of your entire life, loves you enough to die for you, and wants you to be fulfilled in the calling He has for you. He will not take away the gift He has given to you, but neither will He force it on you. His love for you is not the whole picture, however. He also wants you to love and trust Him because that, and really that alone, is the foundation of your fulfilling God's life calling for you. Therefore, it is essential that you have a choice in life, for love and trust are always a choice. If the choice is removed, so is the love. If you have no choice, you have no trust.

All of us are born for a reason, and in a time and place of God's choosing. Your parents may not have planned for you to come when you did, but you are no accident. If you have the right lenses, you may also see that you were born to a destiny that is better than you ever dreamed. The evidence may be all around you, waiting to be discovered. This destiny is not simply about a job or career. It is a call to follow Jesus into the significance He has ordained for your life, whatever vocation He uses to get you there. His kingdom call transcends occupations and job descriptions. In fact, the call is not just about you. It is about Him and His purposes— He is not some high-in-the-sky career counselor with a wonderful plan for your own personal life. You will not regret the plans He has forged for your life, but it is not all about your own personal happiness and fulfillment. The purpose of God for your life is much more than that.

Discovering Your Destiny

God's fingerprints are on your early life, but most of us cannot see them until we look back in hindsight. J. Robert Clinton refers to this young phase of our lives as our "sovereign foundations." We really do not have control over the factors that shape us at this stage of development, any more than we can choose our parents. There really is no reason to describe a leader at this phase (as I will do for the other phases to follow), since no one reading this book is likely in this stage, and those in this stage rarely lead anyone.

What I can do is help you look back and perhaps recognize that all the factors of your early life were sovereignly designed for a purpose and contributed toward your fulfilling your calling. You can piece together some of the destiny you were prepared to walk into, and maybe you can even start to make sense of your childhood. God can bring healing, redemption, and even meaning to the hardships you have experienced, as difficult as that is to believe. He is not the author of evil or a stranger to suffering. He is big enough to use even the consequences of evil for his own purpose (Proverbs 16:4), with grace and compassion.

Winston Churchill once said, "It is a mistake to try to look too far ahead. The chain of destiny can only be grasped one link at a time." If you are aware of some of the thoughts presented in this book, I hope that as you grasp your destiny one link at a time, you will be able to make more sense of what has occurred in your life and even of some of what is coming your way. Just as Paul's early background doesn't come close to revealing what God would do with him, analysis of your own early life will not reveal your full destiny. It can help, however, to consider some of the ways God can redeem the pain of your life and use those blessings for His purposes. As you continue to walk further on the journeys of your own life, it is good on occasion to reflect on your early days and see if some of the fingerprints of God are more obvious.

Many of us have not recognized the hand of God in our birth and early years. Ambrose Bierce, a satirist and author at the turn of last century, once commented that destiny can be a tyrant's authority for crime and a fool's excuse for failure. There is a little too much truth in that. I do not want to use the idea of destiny to cripple you with fear of making a wrong choice, or to give you the excuse to make all sorts of wrong ones. For the purposes of this book, I simply want you to consider that God may have a reason why your early life was the way it was, and I want to give you the hope of discovering a redemptive purpose. The hand of God may not have been clear while you were in the midst of your child-hood, but in hindsight you may be able to detect His presence at times you felt alone. You may find His purpose in events that seemed insane at the time. You may find His wisdom behind decisions made seemingly in confusion. Finding God's hand at work in our earlier life can help us put to rest some of the issues of our past and may even bring some healing to old wounds.

You can begin by doing an inventory of your early life and taking stock of the factors that influenced you to become the person you are today. This is a healthy way to balance your past and focus your present. These questions may be helpful:

- Why you were born at the time and in the place where God chose to place you?
- What is special about the cultural soil that you emerged from and that you carry with you in every thought and impulse?
- For what purpose might God use the kinds of things that make you excited or sad?
- What good purpose might there be for the childhood you had?

Paul was not someone bound to his past. He did not carry around excess baggage, nor did unhealed wounds slow him down. When he put his hand to the plow, he did not look back (Luke 9:62). It is not healthy to spend much time looking back. We must live in the present, pressing ahead into our future, hearing the voice of our Lord calling us on.

In Philippians 3, Paul lists much of his background, only to say that "forgetting what lies behind and reaching forward to what lies ahead,

I press on toward the goal for the prize of the upward call of God in Christ Jesus" (Philippians 3:13–14). Think of the simple exercises in this chapter as merely looking in the rearview mirror as you face forward, pressing on in your pursuit of Jesus' calling for your life. Paul used his past to identify with his mission field (Acts 22:1–21), to confirm his unique calling in life (Galatians 1:11–24), to demonstrate the radical transformation of his life (1 Timothy 1:14–16), and to motivate himself for his zealous commitment in the present (1 Corinthians 15:8–11; Ephesians 2:1–13). He never saw his past as an excuse for fruitless living in the present.

Here are some factors to consider as you look back over your early life and try to capture a small piece of the destiny God may have for you. Go over each one and make notes on what may have been an important influence in making you the person you are today:

- Family heritage and relatives
- Friends and associates
- Geopolitical and historical events surrounding this time of your life
- Personality traits
- Birth order and siblings
- Cultural persuasions
- Language and education
- Painful and positive memories
- Passions and preferences
- Strengths and weaknesses
- Abilities and vulnerabilities

Next, learn to respond positively to God's purposes and His leading you through your background, without letting them dominate your present or future life with Christ. To move forward into the destiny God has for you, reconciling your past will be essential. Forgive those who hurt you, not for their sake but your own. Even if you don't want to let people off the hook for the evil they have committed, you cannot move forward without setting yourself free from people in your past. By keeping them on the hook, you also keep yourself hooked to your past. Remember, forgiveness is not for those who deserve it but for those who do not. Forgiveness is always substitutionary—it means accepting the evil done to you and releasing any demand for payment. Jesus forgave you, and to walk in His love we must also forgive others and leave justice to God.

It is not just the negative events of your past that you must reconcile. Some people are still living in the memories of their past accomplishments. There are many people who never progress because they are embittered by their past—some because of the glory days and some because of the gory ones. You cannot move forward into significance if you are bound by your past. Paul balanced his past and his present by always pursuing a better future—a future of knowing Christ more fully.

After you have made a list of the influential events, people, and qualities of your childhood, try to place them into the same types of useful categories that Paul himself used. Ask yourself, *How have these events, people, or qualities helped me to . . .*

- Identify with a specific mission field? In what ways have these factors prepared me to reach a certain type of person?
- Confirm my unique call in life? What are the fingerprints of God that shaped me for what He is now calling me to do?
- Perceive God's redemptive love and power? How have these factors told the story of God's love and power in my life?
- Motivate myself for greater service in the present? How have these events, people, and qualities from my past fueled my love and passion for Jesus in the present?

My Destiny

I was born into a family that loved the Pacific Ocean. My father and his brothers loved surfing so much that my uncle became a legendary big-wave rider in Hawaii.[6] Because of this heritage, I became a lifeguard like my father and his father had been. I had no idea at the time, but while I was serving eight years lifeguarding the beaches of Los Angeles, God was giving me lessons that would help me one day to teach people how to make disciples for Christ's kingdom. My book *Search & Rescue* is based on these years of experience lifeguarding.

Before I was even one year old, my mother gave birth to my brother. For decades I had no idea how this had affected my personality, any more than a fish would be aware that it is wet. But looking back many years later, I realized that because my mother had another baby to care for before I was even out of diapers, I became a very independent person. To this day I am quite self-sufficient and able to make do with whatever life hands me. Of course, this independence also presents a weakness in my relationships that I must struggle to overcome.

My father is an artist. I also consider myself an artist. I received my bachelor's degree in art from California State University–Long Beach. My upbringing and my education taught me to think from a creative point of view, which I have taken into serving my Lord. I may not work anymore on canvas or with clay, but I still approach the way I do ministry as an artist, looking for fresh and creative ways to do the important things in church.

In the years before I entered high school, my father struggled with alcoholism. He sobered up when I was in high school, but I still have painful memories of moments when he was not there for me during a particularly formative period of my life. In particular, I often recall the basketball hoop that hung on our garage. It had a slight tilt and was half an inch too high because a ten-year-old boy put it up, without any help, several weeks after Christmas. Unbeknownst to me, my father's virtual absence was creating a hunger in me for a father figure who could teach me what it means to be a man. Eventually the Lord redeemed this painful consequence by placing a desire in me for mentoring relationships with more experienced men. Over the course of my life, I have been blessed tenfold with godly mentors who have shaped my growth and development in many ways. I have also found personal motivation to become a better father to my own son.

My namesake and great-great grandfather, Cornelius Cole, was a U.S. senator from California during the Lincoln administration. He was an abolitionist and had come to California in 1849 to help the state join the Union. He owned a piece of property in southern California that was called Colegrove. He sold it to the City of Los Angeles, and today it is called Hollywood. I never met this man, but I do feel that I inherited something from him besides his name. I too want to set people free from bondage. I also have a sense of ownership about Los Angeles and have always felt called to bring transformation here. We are now beginning to see many new churches in Hollywood, and I always think of my namesake as I coach some of the church planters. I want to take that place back, but for God's kingdom, not my own possession.

The Cole family is full of overachievers. Not only was my great-great grandfather a senator, my grandfather was a Colonel in the U.S. Marine Corps as well as a founder of the Devil Pups program. My father is an accomplished animator whose work has won an Oscar, an Emmy, several Clios (the advertising awards), and an Annie lifetime achievement award (an award in the field of animation). Many of my siblings and cousins have advanced academic degrees and work today as doctors, researchers, or lawyers. I must admit that I carry some of this sense of ambition and drive in me as well. I excelled in sports in my younger years and learned that discipline and hard work, applied over the course of a lifetime, will lead to success. I hope that I am no longer striving for my own fame, or for my place in this family, but I remain devoted to hard work and discipline applied in a singular direction.

All these simple examples demonstrate that my upbringing shaped me for a purpose. There is a Designer, and He has been applying the brushstrokes of my life. I could never see this when I was a child, but it makes sense now that I can look back from the vantage point of one who has found peace with God. I can see now how God's hand was on my life before I was even born.

There is a great deal more for you to discover than what you can find in your early years. That period of your life is just the beginning. In the next chapter, we will look at the important developmental phase of inner-life growth. When we do, we will see that a man named Saul had, unknown to himself, a very important and consequential Divine appointment on a certain road to Damascus.

The entrance to Petra with the Treasury in the background.

2

New Life

A Sharp Detour onto a Straight Street

One meets his destiny often on the road he takes to avoid it.
—French Proverb

*And last of all, as to one untimely born, He appeared
to me also. For I am the least of the apostles, and not fit to
be called an apostle, because I persecuted the church of God.
But by the grace of God I am what I am, and His grace
toward me did not prove vain.*
—the apostle Paul (1 Corinthians 15:8–10)

THERE IS ONE MISSIONARY JOURNEY that you won't find pictured in the maps at the back of your Bible. On this journey, a man named Saul, later called Paul, was heading to Damascus.[1] His mission was not to preach the Gospel but to stop others from doing so. He was going not to make disciples but to arrest and imprison them.

I imagine that Saul's day began in normal fashion, without any indication that everything would change for him forever. Do you ever pause in the morning and wonder if this is a day that will alter your life forever? Probably not, but I do on occasion. The truth is that those significant days hit us all at moments, when we least expect them, mixed in as they are with the many days that do not make much of a difference. If only we could foresee them on our calendars—but we cannot. We can live life only by journeying forward, blind to and unaware of the Damascus Road experiences that are coming our way.

Saul's Conversion and New Life

In the Bible's first mention of Saul, we are introduced to him as the one who oversees the execution of a great man of God, Stephen. The day of Stephen's execution would haunt Saul for the rest of his life, shaping his whole being. Later he would wish that it had never happened, but by no means would he ever consider excluding that shameful story from the written chronicle of his life, because it was such an important marker. As dark as the story is, it marks the starting point for Saul's dramatic transformation, and for that reason alone it remains a pivotal story in the book of Acts.

We do not know where Saul was coming from or going to when he came to be involved in Stephen's death. We do know from the spontaneity of the account that Stephen's execution was not an item on his "things to do" list or an appointment in his diary for that day. Somehow he took a detour from whatever he was supposed to be doing and became involved in Stephen's trial.

Perhaps Saul had been wondering why his peers and leaders were allowing the brand-new sect of Christianity such open access to the people of Jerusalem. Maybe he asked himself, "Why don't they crush these fools?" On this subject, he may even have taken issue with his own mentor, Gamaliel, which is often the case when young, immature leaders find that more seasoned veterans are less dogmatic.

Luke tells us, "The word of God kept on spreading; and a number of the disciples continued to increase greatly in Jerusalem" (Acts 6:7). For a man like Saul, who was a black-and-white thinker, this would have been infuriating. He saw himself as being on the right side of things, and this new sect countered his own beliefs, although he may not have known fully in what ways. What was perhaps even more maddening to him is that even some of Jerusalem's leaders were being enticed to join the movement—Luke goes on to say, "And a great many of the priests were becoming obedient to the faith" (Acts 6:7). Saul would have taken any chance to expose this new thing as fraudulent and an enemy of Judaism.

The Stoning of Stephen

Luke describes Stephen and his execution with specific language and detail. It is strange that the martyrdom of the apostle James, the son of Zebedee, is given just one sentence (Acts 12:2), whereas Stephen's death is given more than a whole chapter (and a long one at that). A primary reason for the lengthy description is that this event—Saul's sitting in a position of authority over Stephen's execution—is the first domino to fall, initiating the momentum of everything yet to come in the book of Acts. This day would not just end one man's life and change another's but would also change human history because of the effect it would have on Saul's life. Thus Luke gives us all the details, probably via the eyewitness Saul himself. Stephen is also the first Christian martyr, the first of many who will die for their faith in Jesus.

One of the ways Luke emphasizes the importance of the story is by painting Stephen as Christlike. In fact, in many ways—not to diminish Stephen's martyrdom—Stephen stands in the place of Jesus Himself. In a real sense, as Saul endorses the execution of Stephen, he is also persecuting Jesus. Later, on the road to Damascus, when Saul falls to the ground and is confronted by Jesus in all His glory, Jesus asks Saul, "Why are you persecuting me?" He then identifies Himself as "Jesus whom you are persecuting." Apparently it is not only Luke who is painting Stephen to be like Christ; Jesus Himself sees Stephen that way.

Stephen was indeed an example of Christ in his work, and in his trial and execution. Among the people, he performed wonders and miracles that drew crowds to hear his message (Acts 6:8). His opponents failed miserably to refute him in argument (Acts 6:10). They brought him to the Sanhedrin without cause. As they had done with Jesus, they stirred false witnesses to testify against him (Acts 6:11–13). The accusation against Stephen was the same as that leveled at Jesus—that he would destroy the temple (Acts 6:13–14). Jesus and Stephen were both brought before Caiaphas, the high priest who served until 36 A.D. Stephen, like Jesus, pronounces judgment on his accusers, saying that they, despite their words to the contrary, are just like their forefathers, who murdered the prophets whom God had sent. He tells them that the temple is not fit for God to live in, and that God is bigger than any building made with human hands.

When Jesus was in the same seat of judgment, his accusers asked Him if He was indeed the Messiah. He answered, "You will see the Son of Man sitting at the right hand of the Almighty, and coming with the clouds of heaven" (Mark 14:62; Luke 22:69). And Stephen gazes up from the same seat, likely before the same officials, and remarks, "Behold, I see the heavens opened up and the Son of Man standing at the right hand of God" (Acts 7:56). The words of Jesus, which cemented His own execution, are now being thrown back into the faces of the same accusers. Now they must either admit that they were wrong, and confess to killing the Messiah, or execute this other man. Without delay, and without proper protocol, Stephen is ushered outside the gates, where he is executed. He calls out to his Lord, "Receive my spirit," much as his Lord did not long before His own execution (Luke 23:46). Like Jesus, as Stephen is dying he prays that God will not hold this sin against his executioners (Acts 7:60; see also Luke 23:34).

Somehow, Saul of Tarsus was drawn that day to the public spectacle of Stephen being confronted by the Council of the Sanhedrin. Luke writes that Saul was in "hearty agreement with putting him to death" (Acts 8:1). That moment would launch Saul on a mission to stamp out the followers of the Nazarene. He would finally have his chance to do away with the traitors once and for all. The older leaders of the Sanhedrin were in favor of Saul's enthusiastic agenda, and they let him run with a long leash (Acts 26:9–11). Luke writes, "Saul began ravaging the church, entering house after house, and dragging off men and women, he would put them in prison" (Acts 8:3).

One of the great ironies of Scripture is what happens next. This persecution, instigated by Saul, sends the people of God out into all of Judea and Samaria, where Jesus once instructed his disciples to go (Acts 1:8). Acts 8:1 says that all of the church's followers were scattered by this persecution and left Jerusalem—except the "sent ones" (the apostles). Don't miss the sarcasm here, simply because the translators have used the word *apostles*. Anyone who could read the Greek would have caught it. The ones who were "sent" were the only ones who didn't go.[2]

Thus, even as Saul is lost in a blind and zealous rage to stamp out Christianity, he still has more to do with getting the saints mobilized and starting churches than do the twelve Jerusalem apostles, who seem slow out of the gate when it comes to actually going on the mission they have been sent to fulfill (Acts 1:8). I do not for a moment think that they were deliberately disobedient. I simply think that they lacked the full faith and understanding that would have allowed them to go. They were bound by what they felt were their responsibilities of leadership, and perhaps by an inherited prejudice that they couldn't recognize in themselves. They probably even thought it noble to remain in the heat of persecution.

God used Saul, even in his sin, to mobilize His people for the Great Commission and fulfill His instructions to go not just to Jerusalem but also to all of Judea and Samaria. The Lord would then use Saul's redeemed life—his life as Paul—to extend His kingdom "to the ends of the earth." Even before Saul was redeemed and regenerated, he had more to do with starting churches than did any other person, and his destiny is evident in almost everything he did. God even used Saul's evil actions for good in His kingdom.

We all may feel the guilt of our own sins that put Jesus on the cross. But because Saul stood and watched approvingly over the execution of

Jesus' stand-in, he later, as Paul, had a unique perspective, which motivated him to work tirelessly and suffer greatly for Jesus. In this way, he had a potent connection with Jesus' crucifixion.

A Divine Appointment

In chapter 9 of Acts, Luke says that Saul of Tarsus is "still breathing threats and murder against the disciples of the Lord." Saul requests documents from the Sanhedrin to authorize him to extend the persecution and follow the Christians, who have scattered to other parts of the world. He wants to go after those in Damascus, but one can easily imagine Saul making a few such journeys. Later in life, describing this time, Paul would say: "And as I punished them often in all the synagogues, I tried to force them to blaspheme; and being furiously enraged at them, I kept pursuing them even to foreign cities" (Acts 26:11). Even before he begins following the Way, he is inclined to go on journeys on behalf of his spiritual convictions.

The conversion of Saul is perhaps one of the most pivotal stories in the book of Acts.[3] Luke tells the story once in his own narrative (Acts 9: 1–31) and then twice more (Acts 22:1–21; 26:2–23), when he quotes Paul retelling it (this chapter combines information from all three accounts). In Luke's telling of the story, in Acts, Saul and his companions are traveling in the heat of the day and nearing their destination when a light brighter than the sun suddenly bursts upon them. That the party is traveling on a desert road in the midday heat is an indication of Saul's very determined nature. And the fact that the light of heaven shines brighter than the midday sun shows us how incredibly radiant the Lord is. His real presence makes everything seem immaterial and unreal and causes everything, even the sunlight, to fade into the background. Saul's companions can see the light, but they cannot see the Lord or understand His voice. Saul, however, can both see and hear the Lord. Falling to his knees, Saul hears the voice say: "Saul, Saul, why are you persecuting me? It is hard for you to kick against the goads."[4] Whatever prodding Saul may already have received, until this moment he has rejected it all and proceeded with a clear conscience and determination, fully believing that he has been fulfilling God's will. But finally, when Jesus shows Himself, he gets Saul to pay attention.

Heaven is in hot pursuit of those who are the objects of our Lord's love, even if they fail to recognize it at first. When Jesus wants to, He has a way of getting our attention. Usually that involves asking questions, which is often what He is inclined to do. And when He is particularly disappointed, He will begin the question with the personal name of the one He is addressing. Sometimes he does this twice, to really get the needed attention: "Simon, Simon" (Luke 22:31), "Martha, Martha" (Luke 10:41), even "Jerusalem, Jerusalem" (Luke 13:34). (I often imagine him slowly shaking His head when I have been particularly foolish, and I hear him sigh, "Neil, Neil." Do you ever hear the heavenly echo of your name as well?) In Luke's story, it is "Saul, Saul" (Acts 9:4). There is not going to be any way for Saul to ignore the Lord's guidance at this point. In addition to showing him the blinding light and speaking to him in a loud voice, the risen Christ gets Saul's attention by addressing him in Aramaic (Acts 26:14).[5]

Jesus tells Saul to continue on to Damascus, where he will receive instructions concerning all he has been appointed to do. When Saul rises from the ground, he is blind. What a contrast—from seeing a light brighter than the sun to stumbling in darkness. One moment he is able to see but spiritually blind; now he is physically blind but can finally see spiritual things with clarity. Saul's companions help him get to the city, and they find a place to stay in a house owned by a man named Judas. The house is on a street called Straight. Saul stays there for three days, still blind, without eating or drinking.

Imagine what must have been going on in Saul's head after he encountered Jesus, on the heels of overseeing the deaths and imprisonment of several of His people (Acts 26:10). In less than two minutes, his entire life and all he had lived for were turned upside down, and the Lord gave him three solid days to let this event sink in. I wonder what Saul thought about during those three long days. Did he begin to doubt the experience, thinking that perhaps he had simply suffered a sudden aneurism and hallucinations combined with blindness? Or was it a bizarre case of sunstroke? I doubt that Saul entertained such thoughts for very long, if they did come, for he had a vision that Ananias would come and heal him of his blindness.[6] Besides, that life-defining moment, along with Jesus' voice and the vision—all of it was indelibly etched on his memory and could be recalled in all its graphic detail. So he sat waiting and wondering, listening and praying, and all the time fasting.

Maybe Saul thought that from this point on he would obey this Jesus, even if that meant sitting in the dark in this strange house for the rest of his days. The Lord did say that He would tell him what he must do, and so Saul must have reasoned that there was a plan. He must have wondered, "What can I do, now that I am blind?" Did he have hope that the one who healed blind people could heal him? I imagine he felt that he didn't deserve to be healed. Did he anticipate that the Lord would have further punishment for him beyond the blindness? All this time, thinking he had been doing the right thing, he had been an enemy of the Lord and His work. Saul knew what the Lord of Hosts in the Scriptures would have done to those who opposed His will. I wonder how many times Saul replayed in his mind the words of Stephen, and the death by stoning that followed. I imagine that Saul spent considerable time going over in his mind all the Old Testament passages about the Messiah, and that he saw them in a new light. Perhaps the Lord had given him a vision of Ananias healing him in answer to some of his grave doubts, and to keep him out of the dark pit of self-condemnation. Saul had much to think about in those three days sitting alone in the dark. Like Jesus in a tomb for three days before he was raised, Saul spent three days in darkness awaiting his new life.

Eventually a powerful confirmation of his new calling came to him and permanently removed any room for doubt. Saul heard his name spoken once again in Aramaic, only this time it was not repeated in seeming disapproval but coupled with the endearing term "Brother." Ananias came to him, laid his hands on him in support and warmth, and said, "Brother Saul, the Lord Jesus, who appeared to you on the road by which you were coming, has sent me so that you may regain your sight and be filled with the Holy Spirit." Ananias laid hands on Saul and said, "Brother Saul, receive your sight!" Immediately the scales fell from Saul's eyes, and he could see again. We later learn (Galatians 1:1) that he received a prophetic word from the Lord that would reveal a life calling. Try to imagine the gravity of this moment—not only is Jesus not Saul's avowed enemy, He also has a plan for Saul. And the plan is incredible. Saul, writing later as Paul, recounts the words spoken to him through Ananias: "The God of our fathers has appointed you to know His will and to see the Righteous One and to hear an utterance from His mouth. For you will be a witness for Him to all men of what you have seen and heard. Now why do you delay? Get up and be baptized, and wash away your sins, calling on His name."

The prophetic word, the healing, and the mercy and forgiveness Saul had received must have renewed his body. Immediately Saul arose, and in spite of his three days without food or water he went with Ananias to the Abana River, which flowed just outside the city's northern wall, and Ananias baptized him. I feel it is significant that the great apostle Paul was baptized by a man barely known in the Scriptures. Ananias, a faithful but common man, was chosen as the Lord's vessel to restore Saul, heal him, baptize him, and announce his new calling. There was not a laying on of hands by any of the twelve apostles. Jesus came to Saul through the hands of a simple man otherwise unknown to history. But that's the point. It is the presence of Jesus that makes any of us special for His service, whether we are one of the twelve apostles, Ananias, Saul, or just ourselves.

No matter how dramatic your calling is when Jesus speaks to you, confirmation from a secondary source is always appreciated. Jesus doesn't mind confirming such things, because they are important to remember for the rest of your life, and He does know how easily we can be deceived. Saul's doubts and fears were laid to rest in a moment, when a man he had never met called him "Brother." One moment he may have been wondering if he would ever know what was going on. The next moment, a man clearly directed by the Lord arrived where Saul was hiding. The man somehow knew what Saul had seen and heard from the Lord on the road coming into town. The man's name was the same as that of the man Saul had seen come to him in a vision. Then, to establish once and for all that this was from God, the man laid hands on Saul and healed his blindness. Finally, after all this dramatic confirmation, he told Saul his destiny and gave him his new orders.

Paul Begins

Saul didn't delay in his new calling. He showed up at the same synagogue where he was supposed to go, but his authority and his orders had changed radically. What a surprise it must have been for those who had come expecting the notorious Saul of Tarsus (Acts 9:13; 26:11), enemy of the Way, and instead heard the same man affirming that Jesus is the Son of God. Saul got busy fast. The same determination and zealousness that had made him the persecutor of the church he now put in service to it. He stayed some time in Damascus, preaching in the synagogues, and he probably traveled to Arabia during this season while maintaining Damascus as his base (Galatians 1:17).

Many speculate that he went off to Arabia to be alone with God and have his theology straightened out. Personally, I find that hard to believe, knowing the passionate determination of this young man (now in his mid-thirties). He was told that he would preach the Gospel, and I believe that is what he set out to do. Right from the start, the Bible says, he "kept increasing in strength and confounding the Jews who lived at Damascus by proving that this Jesus is the Christ." I believe that he worked out his new faith in the best possible place—not in Arabia, but in obedience, doing the work. I like to think that he probably visited the incredible city carved out of stone, called Petra, which was the capital of the Nabataeans. The legend is that Aaron was buried in the mountains of this place, and there would have been a synagogue and Jews living there, so he would likely have ventured down, preaching the Gospel he had come to love and live. It is not that isolation and reflection were not an important part of Saul's development. I just imagine that he would not have volunteered for such a respite, especially at such a young age, and at this early stage. The time of being alone and listening was to come, but, as is the case for most of us, it had to be forced on him by the removal of all other options.

Rejection in Arabia, Damascus, and Jerusalem

Whatever he was doing in Damascus and Arabia, he got the Gentile authorities upset, and I can hardly imagine that his quietly sitting on a rock in the desert listening to God would have done that. According to his own recounting, the ethnarch under Aretas IV, king of the Nabataeans (Arabia), was guarding the city gates of Damascus to try to capture Saul and kill him. Luke tells us that it was once again the Jews who may have stirred up this persecution, probably by instigating some sort of unrest, which set the Gentile law of the land after Saul. But Saul found out.

In a dramatic escape, Saul was let down in a basket through a window in the wall of the city, to sneak away under cover of night. It is possible that this was three years into his new faith (Galatians 1:18), and that he was already a "basket case." His newfound faith, adrenaline, youthful passion, and naiveté could take him only so far. He was being chased out of town for the first time, but certainly not the last.

Once again he was on the Damascus road, but this time heading in the opposite direction. I wonder how long he paused over the spot on that road where his new life had begun. It is close to the city where he was a wanted man, and so perhaps even under cover of night he didn't have time to reflect on what he must have viewed as a sort of holy ground—a place that held a special but haunting place in his heart.

Having offended not only the Jews but also the Gentiles that he had been called to reach, Saul returned to Jerusalem to get to know the spiritual fathers of the church. If he was not welcome in Damascus and Arabia, imagine how cold his reception must have been in Jerusalem. Those who were once his friends were now his enemies, and those who were once his enemies could hardly be friendly after all he had done to them and their community. I can see why it took him three years and the threat of capture and death to muster the courage to return.

He tried to establish fellowship with the disciples, but they wanted nothing to do with him and were afraid of him. His old associates probably were even less welcoming. He must have felt as if he didn't have a friend in the world, and although he understood that this was his own doing, he still must have felt the sting of loneliness.

It was at that moment, when all seemed to turn their backs on him, that he met a friend who would leave a lasting mark on his life. He is called by his brothers and sisters, the "son of encouragement" or Barnabas. I like the way the New American Standard Bible says it: "But Barnabas *took hold of him* and brought him to the apostles and described to them how he had seen the Lord on the road, and that he had talked to him, and how at Damascus he had spoken out boldly in the name of Jesus" (emphasis added).

When Saul was alone in Damascus, a friend named Ananias had come and laid hands on him with a message of hope. In Jerusalem, when he was again alone and alienated, another friend laid hands on him and welcomed him. There is nothing quite like the warm touch of a friend in a lonely situation. Barnabas, as described in Acts, seems uniquely gifted to read people and see the true light in their souls. He also seems to know exactly what they need, and he loves to lift their spirits and draw out what good things he sees in them. This quality is such a part of his life that the people of the Jerusalem church have changed his name from Joseph to Barnabas, which literally means "son of encouragement" (Acts 4:36). What a special kind of person he is—we need more of them.

Saul spoke with Peter and James and set out to start his new ministry in Jerusalem. There was only one place he could go to start this new work—the synagogue where Stephen had once preached. Saul may have felt bound to reconcile his past mistakes as quickly as he could, and so he took up the work of the man he had helped to kill.

What seems like a wonderful plan, however, is most often not what happens. In little more than two weeks (Galatians 1:18), Saul was once again on a journey. Since he was seen as a traitor, his work among the Hellenistic Jews was even less well received than Stephen's had been (Acts 9:29). The Lord appeared to Saul while he was in the temple and said, "Make haste, and get out of Jerusalem quickly, because they will not accept your testimony about Me" (Acts 22:18). When the Lord says, "Make haste" and "quickly" in the same sentence, I suspect it means "Head for the door now, and don't pack any bags!" But Saul tried to convince the Lord of his own usefulness in Jerusalem. It may well be that he was hoping that if he stayed, he would have a chance to make up for what he had done to Stephen. This wasn't an argument he could win.

The Lord said to him, emphatically, "Go! For I will send you away to the Gentiles." In other words, "Your calling is mine to decide, and you are not called to reconcile your past. I already did that. Get moving!"

I always chuckle when I see the beauty of God in how He decides people's destinies. He chose Peter, a lowly fisherman without any theological training whatsoever, to be the apostle to the Jews. Matthew, the hated tax collector who would have been considered a traitor to his people, was chosen to write the Gospel account for the Jews. Then He found a strict, well-educated Pharisee to be His apostle to communicate the Gospel *to the Gentiles*. Most of us, apparently including Saul, would have thought that the Pharisees were the ones best prepared to preach to the Jews, but this is a human way of seeing things. Jesus saw things very differently and said, "I will send you away to the Gentiles." In Christ, the things that once were considered our greatest strengths become our weaknesses, and the things that we once considered weaknesses are turned into strengths. In all of this, it is the power and presence of Jesus that makes the difference, not our own education, experience, or excellence.

Benched in Tarsus

The disciples sent Saul from Jerusalem to Caesarea, then on to Tarsus. He had been rejected in Damascus, and now he was rejected in Jerusalem. All he could do was head home to Tarsus, where he spent the next ten years. He must have felt defeated. He must have felt the way any great athlete does when he is sent to the bench while the game is on.

There is no mention in the Bible of Saul's family except that he had a sister and nephew (Acts 23:16) and a woman who was like an adopted mother (Romans 16:13). So what was waiting for him when he retuned home?

As Jesus once commented, a prophet's hometown and own people are usually the most resistant to the prophet's message. I'm sure that was the case here as well; that is the only way to account for the five times Saul was scourged by the Jews before he wrote 2 Corinthians, in 56 A.D. I am sure Saul preached the Gospel any chance he got, and he may even have started churches (Galatians 1:21; Acts 15:23, 41), but a decade in one place would have been a long time for this "sent one." Many speculate that it was in Arabia that Saul sat and listened to the Lord about the important things concerning his life and faith (Galatians 1:11–12), but I believe it was while he was sidelined in Tarsus that Jesus tutored him and prepared him to fulfill his destiny.

Tarsus was a good place to be stationed if you were to learn how to evangelize the Gentiles, for it was a renowned cultural center for teaching philosophy, rhetoric, and law. There would be days to come when Paul would pour out all that he had bottled up within himself (Philippians 2:17), but these days in Tarsus were about receiving the lessons that would eventually be necessary. In this town where he had once learned languages, his sacred heritage as one of God's chosen people, and the Holy Writ, he now was to learn pagan culture, philosophy, and rhetorical skills, which would serve him well in his future journeys. Surely he had intuitively picked up a lot as a child in this town, but during this decade he was a highly motivated student because now he had been called by Jesus to reach the Gentile world. One couldn't find a better place for this education. Later, in his writings, he would quote Menander, Aratus, and the Cretan poet Epimenides. In his speech to the stoic philosophers in Athens, he used apt allusions to Aeschylus's *Eumenides* and to Plato's *Phaedo,* and he made a tactful paraphrase of Plato's *Republic.*[7]

I don't think he would have been sent to Tarsus if he hadn't had a place to return to. I imagine that family members who had been so devoted to raising a strict Pharisee would not have been open to the new Christian sect. They might have viewed his new life as a betrayal, and he would likely have been seen as a traitor. Perhaps by this time his father had passed away and his mother was more accepting of her son's faith. Or there is a chance that both his parents had died, and he was simply moving into his own inheritance. Another possibility is that his parents were still in Jerusalem, where his sister and her family lived, and he was simply using his family's home in their absence. He would later refer to another Christian woman as his adopted mother, and so perhaps he was without his own mother at this dark time in his life. Is it possible that he had lost his wife and child as well as his parents in an earlier tragedy? All we really know is that he had a place to stay, and that the Jerusalem disciples sent him there.

Those ten years in Tarsus are a glaring gap in Saul's story. We can assume a few things to fill in some of the story. In 56 A.D., when he wrote 2 Corinthians, Paul recounts many of the sufferings he endured for the sake of Christ, the majority of which do not appear in Acts, and so perhaps some of them occurred during his ten-year sojourn in the region of his hometown.

In that second letter to the Corinthians, Paul says that he received thirty-nine lashes from the Jews on five different occasions.[8] None of these instances are recorded in Acts, and so it is safe to assume that some occurred during those ten years. He was brought to the point of death in this manner five times. He would later write to the Galatians, "I bear on my body the brand-marks of Jesus" (Galatians 6:17). It is unfathomable how someone could endure this severe pain more than once, let alone five times. What could possibly compel a man to bear such suffering?

This type of scourging was sometimes meant to purge and restore a brother to the synagogue instead of making him suffer excommunication. The punishment was executed by three or more leaders called the *bet dîn,* or house of judges, and was exercised for a number of reasons given in the Mishnah; Makkoth 3:1–9 lists several reasons for this punishment, including being a false teacher and entering the temple unclean, both of which Paul would be accused of having done.[9] Saul saw the synagogues as strategically important for the mission he was ultimately called to fulfill, and so perhaps he chose to be beaten raw in this way just to maintain his access. He could have escaped this horrendous suffering by being excommunicated or keeping his mouth shut, but neither was a real option for him, and so instead he endured.

There was a statement in oral law (Talmud) that if a sinner broke certain commandments twice and was sentenced for both infractions, he was to suffer the first punishment, heal, and then be scourged a second time.[10] Perhaps this is how Saul came to suffer so many of these punishments, all so that he could continue to preach the Gospel to the people he loved so much.[11] After one is scourged in this way, one is to be treated again as family and allowed access to the synagogue.

He would later say to the Romans that he was willing to go much farther than this—that he would even go to hell for the sake of his countrymen. He says, "I am telling the truth in Christ, I am not lying, my conscience testifies with me in the Holy Spirit, that I have great sorrow and unceasing grief in my heart. For I could wish that I myself were accursed, separated from Christ for the sake of my brethren, my kinsmen according to the flesh" (Romans 9: 1–3). This love for people who would continue to punish him is not normal—not human, but divine. It is the love of Christ, who also endured lashes and crucifixion for those who hated him. Saul/Paul eventually would even write that he fulfilled the sufferings of Christ (Colossians 1:24).

Every time Saul preached the Gospel in the synagogues, he did so knowing full well the punishment he might have to endure—perhaps inflicted upon him by the very elders who had once taught him as a child. I imagine he weighed the cost and many times preached anyway. He truly loved his enemies, his own people. Perhaps he received a scourging for preaching the Gospel, and then afterward preached again, and that he then received two more punishments, with some healing time in between.

From this we can see how much Saul loved the Jews and how much he was willing to go through for Jesus. His suffering was in every way premeditated and fully informed.

Somehow, in the gaps that Luke and the epistles leave us, Saul was shipwrecked three times and spent a night and a day floating in the ocean.[12] He received two additional beatings with rods, events not found in Acts. All of this happened sometime before 56 A.D., when he wrote his second epistle to the Corinthians. These events must fit somewhere in the holes not filled in by Acts. It is likely that during these difficult days Saul kept trying to do the work and met disaster after disaster, all as preparation for the work that would come, eventually.

This was Saul's graduate school, his training for future deployment. Local legend says that he retreated into the hills of Taurus, to a cave where he received the special revelation of the third heaven mentioned in 2 Corinthians 12:1–10. This timing would match the time frame presented in that passage. There is even a cave in the mountains that is said to be that special place, but this assertion is in no way verifiable, and so it is pointless speculation. In any case, whenever and wherever Saul received this revelation, there is no doubt that during those stressful and difficult years in Tarsus he was being taught by Jesus. He would say to the Galatians, "For I would have you know, brethren, that the Gospel which was preached by me is not according to man. For I neither received it from man, nor was I taught it, but I received it through a revelation of Jesus Christ" (Galatians 1:11–12).

Compared to the exciting first three years of his Christian life, these ten years must have seemed like a prison sentence, full of suffering and rejection. We never really hear of great fruitfulness from these years, although there are reports of churches in this area a few years later (Acts 15:41). There would eventually be some lasting fruit from this period, but it appears that this time was more about getting stuff into Saul than getting stuff out of him. But it took only ten years for Paul to establish self-sufficient reproducing church movements in five entire provinces of the Roman Empire—Galatia, Macedonia, Achaia, Asia, and Illyricum— and so this decade in Syria and Cilicia must have seemed slow and difficult indeed.

While Saul was "on the bench," the real game continued to play out. The Gospel broke out among the Gentiles. First Peter was led by the Lord to share the Gospel with Cornelius and his household (Acts 10–11). As word of that spread, a new church was started in Syrian Antioch (Acts 11:18–20). These "Christians," as the locals called them, intentionally turned to the Gentiles to preach the Gospel. To encourage this venture of faith and obedience the Lord blessed the work with rapid and dramatic growth.

The apostles back in Jerusalem, hearing about this fast growth, sent the trusted leader Barnabas to scout out what was going on. Barnabas was truly excited and blessed by what he saw, but he soon left Antioch on a journey of his own. Barnabas probably remembered the young man he had found alone in Jerusalem, and how God had called that young man to preach the Gospel to the Gentiles. He also remembered the young man's short stint in Jerusalem, and that he had been shipped home after only two weeks. Somehow, he knew in his heart that this was perfect for Saul, and so, believing that God wanted Saul involved in Antioch, Barnabas went to Tarsus to call him back into action.

Luke says, "He left for Tarsus to look for Saul; and when he had found him, he brought him to Antioch." By this time Saul may have been traveling in the region preaching the Gospel or floating in the sea after another shipwreck, or he may have been in his cave, hearing from God. In any case, once he heard this invitation from Barnabas, he did not delay in going to Antioch. He was ready to get back in the game, after a decade on the bench.

Probably in his early forties by now, Saul was better prepared for what lay ahead of him. That is not to say that Saul had learned all he needed to; as we will see, he still had much to learn. But it does mean that he had learned all he could in the classroom of Tarsus.

Back in the Game

Antioch, on the Orontes River, sixteen miles from the Mediterranean, was at that time the third largest city in the Roman Empire. Only Rome and Alexandria were bigger. Together, Barnabas and Saul worked for a year serving this young and rapidly growing church. I imagine that there was a synergy among its members that can only be explained as the presence of Christ working through a small band of leaders completely devoted to Christ. The Jerusalem church seemed encumbered with a leadership team of twelve apostles, a group of elders (some speculate up to seventy, led by James), and the remaining Hellenistic Jewish leaders, called The Seven, caring for their own people.[13] In contrast, the church in Antioch had five leaders of varying backgrounds, all serving with great faith and simple obedience.

An example of how quickly decisions can be made with a small, agile team is how they responded as a church when they heard the prophetic news of an impending famine in Jerusalem. Without delay, they sold what they could to collect an offering for Barnabas and Saul to take to the saints there. Enough time had passed that the church in Antioch must have felt that Saul would be safe going to Jerusalem, especially carrying a gift for famine relief. That would be true this time, but not necessarily in the future. The next time he came back to Jerusalem with gifts for relief, he was attacked by a mob. But we are getting ahead of ourselves.

The time of this first journey back to Jerusalem was critical for the new movement. The first of the twelve apostles was martyred. James, the son of Zebedee, was executed. Peter was also arrested and, if not for a dramatic rescue by angelic Special Forces, he too would have been killed. Not long after that, King Herod, who had sanctioned these attacks and accepted worship as if he himself were a deity, was struck down and died, and again a period of peaceful expansion was granted to the church in Jerusalem.

It is possible that during this stay in Jerusalem Saul had private counsel with Peter, James, and John about the revelation he had received and his calling to go to the Gentiles.[14] It is also possible that the revelation he received was the one he talks about cryptically in 2 Corinthians 12, but it seems that it also had something to do with preaching the Gospel to the Gentiles without their need to first become Jews. The leaders of the new church gave Barnabas and Saul the right hand of fellowship and sent them on their way to begin their mission to the Gentiles, just as Peter had been commissioned to reach the Jews.

Having completed their mission, Barnabas and Saul returned to Antioch. This time, Saul had no qualms about leaving Jerusalem and may have been anxious to return to the vibrant Antioch church, composed of both Gentiles and Jews. Even though they left the financial gift behind, they did not come back empty-handed. They brought John Mark with them.

Contributing to the Team

Once he was back in Antioch, Saul was with this special team of leaders made up of five "prophets and teachers." Barnabas is mentioned first, and Saul last. I would not be quick to assume that the list is in order of prominence or importance. More likely it is simply following the order of prophets mentioned first, and teachers last. Saul does call himself a teacher a couple of times, much later in life (1 Timothy 2:7; 2 Timothy 1:11), and so perhaps this is the role he filled while in Antioch. Barnabas, who was a Jew from Cyprus, was an encourager or exhorter and may very well have been a prophet. Both Barnabas and Saul are called apostles once they are actually sent out, but a team made up of an apostle and a prophet to lay a strong foundation (Ephesians 2:20) was very important, and Barnabas and Saul may have filled those roles ideally, as Paul and Silas would have done, too (Silas, before being sent, is also referred to as a prophet).

Simeon, who was called Niger, is the next mentioned. Simeon is a Jewish name, and Niger is Latin, meaning "black." He may have had darker skin and may have had African origins. Some scholars believe that this Simeon is the Simon of Cyrene who was forced to help Jesus carry his cross. But he is not said to be from Cyrene, which is in North Africa, though Lucius, who is mentioned in the same sentence, is singled out as being from Cyrene. If he is the same Simon of Cyrene, father of Alexander and Rufus, then his son Rufus may be the one mentioned in Romans 16:13, where Paul also refers to Rufus's mother as his own. It could be that Saul stayed in their home while in Antioch and was adopted into the family. Perhaps Simeon came from a predominantly Roman part of the empire, or perhaps his Latin name (Niger) just seemed more fitting for him, and so he is called "black."

Lucius of Cyrene is also a Latin name, and there is a possibility that he is the Lucius mentioned as having accompanied Paul while he was writing Romans (Romans 16:21). Manaen was an elderly statesman whose name was a Greek form of a Hebrew name (Menahem), which means "comforter." He is said to have grown up in the inner circle of Herod the Tetrarch, also called Herod Antipas, who famously executed John the Baptist and met with Jesus to mock Him during His trial. Herod Antipas was the youngest son of Herod the Great, the one who had tried to kill Jesus as a small child by slaughtering all the firstborn sons in Bethlehem. This could be quite a story in itself—two childhood friends who, because of choices made along their own journeys, ended up on vastly different sides in a great spiritual war. Last, but certainly not least, Saul is mentioned without any other description, since none would have been necessary.

This unique team of leaders with varied cultural backgrounds was brought together at a unique time, and in a special place, to change the world. Here are a few of the reasons why I believe that this band of leaders was so important and rose to a leading role in the expansion of the kingdom:

1. They represented much more varied cultural expressions than their Jerusalem counterparts.[15]
2. They were a small enough band that even with such varied points of view they could find consensus.

3. They were not a team made up of only one type of spiritual gift but were prophets and teachers (although there would soon be apostles in their midst), and that brought a healthier balance of spiritual input.

4. They devoted time to fasting and praying together to listen to the Lord and to serve Him.

5. They began with an openness to reach all people, not only Jews, and God honored that faith. In the book of Galatians, Paul seems to indicate that they usually shared meals together, both Jew and Gentile. While Peter had initially broken down the barrier of Jew and Gentile, none had the kind of bold interaction yet that was exhibited here. The members of this church shook up the order of the world they knew, and they showed that they were more committed to following the Lord than to following their own Jewish tradition. They were not bound by their cultural walls but were free to think outside the box and love all people. The theological and cultural prejudice that bound the Jerusalem church was not found on this team—that is, until some of the Jerusalem leaders showed up later and infected them (Galatians 2:11–21).

With this team of prophets and teachers, Saul once again heard the voice of the Lord calling him to his mission. While they were serving the Lord, fasting and praying, they all heard the Holy Spirit say, "Set apart for me Barnabas and Saul for the work I have called them to." Try to imagine how this moment felt to Saul. It was like the coach turning to him, nodding, and saying, "Okay, now is your moment. You are ready—go get 'em."

In my experience, I have found that some contexts are best for hearing the voice of the Lord.[16] A small band of leaders such as this one was something special. It became a home base for Saul for much of his adult life. It was in this place that a new and unprecedented work was about to be launched. But that is for the next chapter.

Lessons of Inner-Life Development

At this stage of leadership formation, the leader is usually anxious to be useful, whereas the Lord is less interested in that, since as He is preparing the leader for future work. This stage is often filled with waiting, isolation, even frustration and a sense of abandonment. This is actually a very formative stage of development, where listening to the Lord and obedience are built into the leader in a very practical manner. There are some lessons that a leader can learn only while sitting on the bench.

The main thrust of this phase is to know God in a more personal and dynamic way. From the moment human beings first sinned in the garden, God has been pursuing us. In this important developmental stage, one awakens to this pursuit. A dramatic surrender is characteristic of this phase, whether that is a first-time conversion, a step into greater devotion and life service, or both. For leaders who continue to journey into increasing significance, all the way to a strong finish, this stage of development is characterized by recognizing and surrendering to God's overtures into their lives. Learning to listen to, hear, and obey the voice of the Lord is the lesson most essential for this journey and is foundational for all journeys to follow. This is the start of a relationship that will be the spark and the mark for the rest of the leader's life.

All other stages of life are predicated on learning to hear God's voice and respond in faith and obedience. As I continue to recount the types of lessons learned in this phase of development, you will notice that all share one common element—getting our attention so that we can follow the Lord's leading.

Many of us, like Saul, have grown up in a religion that takes God's word and obeys it without hearing the actual voice that speaks it. God's word is truth. It is pure. It sanctifies us and enlightens us, but it is possible to simply see it as a bounded list of commands to obey rather than as a living and active voice. Saul knew how to read, interpret, and apply the scriptures. This can result in lifeless behavior codification rather than an inner spiritual transformation. What Saul didn't know was how to hear God's active voice in them. Despite constant time spent with the Scriptures, God had to shout at him on the road to Damascus to be heard the first time. In essence, the heart of this stage of life was learning to walk in intimacy with God, hearing and depending on God's leading rather than simply living in conformity to the rules in the book. God's word is more than a book written thousands of years ago. God is alive now and speaks to us in power and intimacy. We must learn to hear his voice and follow it courageously.

Radical Salvation

Life's regrets often shape what we become. While all past sins are forgiven with the redemption that comes in Christ, there are some things we do that leave permanent marks on our lives. Wounds heal, but the scars that stay with us characterize some of this stage of life. In the case of

Saul, he would live every day remembering Stephen's words. God worked in remarkable ways though Saul because of this truth, which at times even seemed to haunt Saul. Those scars could be redeemed for a higher purpose, but they did not just go away. Like the former addict who has a heart to reach other addicts, we may find that the things we have done and been forgiven for at this stage of life can set an agenda for the rest of our lives.

It is important that we realize that all followers of Christ are radically saved. There is no other kind of salvation. Often those who were raised by Christian parents and have always made good moral decisions feel as if their salvation is less dramatic than that of drug dealers or prostitutes who find Christ when they are at the end of their rope. This is a lie. Every salvation is a radical transference from a kingdom of darkness into a kingdom of light, with all that entails. This radical transformation of the soul is truly the energy that propels all of one's spiritual formation and resulting significance. True significance does not come from better strategies or further education; it comes from a life changed by the power of the Gospel.

If you accepted the offer of salvation as a small child and repented of the sin of throwing sand in the sandbox, there is absolutely no reason to suffer from "testimony envy" when you hear the dramatic story of the ex-convict who is now preaching the Gospel. Your salvation is as profound as anyone else's and was purchased at the same extreme cost. God is the same to you as he is to the former alcoholic who now serves Christ. You have been saved from the same just penalty as anyone else who has been forgiven by Christ.

If you are concerned that your story is not as dramatic, it is not your parents' fault, and I do not recommend that you go out and sin so that you too can have a better story. If your life is sedentary and lacking in compelling stories of God's deliverance, it is because you are not taking enough risks for the sake of the Gospel. If you step out on the thin ice of risk so that God must intervene to demonstrate his love and provision for you, then you too will have great stories to tell of God's deliverance.

Destiny Revelation

Occasionally at this stage of life, as happened with Saul, one receives a destiny revelation. Clinton defines this as "significant acts, people, or providential circumstances or timing that hint at some future or special significance to a life and add to an awareness of a sense of destiny in a life."[17] Not every leader experiences a destiny revelation, but when someone does, it is usually at this stage of life. The revelation will not be specific, and the leader will still need to stumble along in the lessons of life's journeys, just like anyone else. The destiny revelation, however, usually holds some promise of future significance that helps the emerging leader get through the struggles.

Like any other kind of prophetic word, a destiny revelation will always carry more weight when accompanied by two or three independent witnesses who can confirm it as being from the Lord. Another type of confirmation is when the word is delivered in a remarkable and supernatural fashion, as was the case with Saul. The fact that Ananias knew who and where Saul was and what had occurred on the road, and then proceeded to heal him of his blindness, as the Lord had ordered, is clear confirmation. The fact that Saul had already received a vision of this occurrence is even more compelling evidence that the message received was indeed from the Lord. In the absence of such confirmation, it's wise to hold any prophetic word loosely. God does know how to communicate, and when He does so, He wants you to understand. He will have no trouble at all confirming His word to you if you are open to it, but many lives have been sidelined by the absence of sound confirmation.

Foundations of Character

At this stage, the leader begins serving in some sort of ministry and has some type of training, either formal or informal. The leader-to-be learns on the job, through practice, and often does not achieve the success he or she desires. The truth is that in your earlier phases of development, God is not so interested in getting stuff out of you. He is intent on getting stuff into you. The first several stages of leadership formation are more about investing in future journeys than they are about experiencing great success early on. Sometimes we are saved from the very success we have been praying for in the early years. If God answered all our prayers at this stage, we would not have the foundation for far greater success in the future. I often feel sadness when I see athletes, rock stars, and movie stars who peak in their early twenties. Imagine what it would be like to be twenty-two years old and have to come to terms with the fact that your best years are behind you, that the next fifty or more years will be all downhill. No wonder so many fall prey to drugs and alcohol, to numb the pain of such a revelation.

Character development is much more important at this stage than ministry skills or knowledge. The lessons in skills and knowledge are also important (and emerging leaders acquire them), but this stage is much more about developing and defining the leader's character. What you *do* is less important than who you *are,* because who you are will determine the things that you do.

Because this stage is more focused on character formation than on ministry success, it is usually accompanied by early tests of the emerging leader's readiness for future journeys. These tests are checks of integrity, of obedience to what God asks, and of the ability to hear and discern God's word. If leaders do well with the tests, they will move forward into other journeys. If not, they will experience the same lessons again, with fiercer pressure. The Chinese philosopher Mencius once noted, "Before a man can do things, there must be things he will not do." These tests are not because God doesn't already know what is in store for the leader, or what is in him or her. These checks are to make clear to the leader what is in him or her, and what is important. They are a chance for the leader to decide that there is a limit to how far he or she can bend as a man or woman of God. A proper response to God's teaching and testing will result in greater responsibility and significance. It is one thing for a leader to trust God. It is an even greater thing when God can trust the leader, and that takes some testing and training earlier in life.

Isolation

Even superstars sit on the bench for a time. When we are young, we have no idea what we do not know. We tend to think we can do anything, and we are ignorant about how unprepared we actually are. God, in his infinite love and wisdom, often removes all options so that we are forced to wait and learn as we receive the investment necessary for future work.

Clinton calls this an "isolation process item." This is where the emerging leader is somehow removed from ministry, usually for an extended time, so that he or she experiences God in a new and/or deeper way. This can be quite frustrating and would not normally be a leader's choice, which is why it is usually thrust upon him or her in a way that is not calculated or anticipated. This isolation feels like punishment, but it is not. It is a calling to listen, learn, and lean on God. It is an investment in future success. It is a deepening of the leader's relationship with God so that the rest of the journeys are marked by this important intimacy. If a leader cannot learn how to learn at this stage, then the other journeys will be put on hold. When the time is right, and the lessons of isolation are learned, God makes that known. My good friend Dezi Baker calls this isolation experience "the long and lonely road." Most find that they are brought out of isolation as suddenly and unexpectedly as they began their lonely trials. And the lessons learned can serve a leader for the rest of his or her life. One does not emerge from the long, lonely road the same as one entered it.

While struggling through the tough lessons of this phase of development, the emerging leader is usually frustrated and aggrieved. In hindsight, after the lessons are learned and applied, the leader will have warm affection for the memories of the tough times. It doesn't do the emerging leader a lot of good for more experienced leaders to proclaim the lessons they themselves learned at this stage, complete with tales of struggles in isolation and frustration, as if sharing these stories will make the younger leader's struggles less painful. It won't. It is far more helpful to feel emerging leaders' pain with them, listen to their stories, and be understanding of and empathetic toward their hurts.

I remember well a meeting I had with a senior pastor when I was in this difficult period of growth. I had to work several jobs to support a young family, all the while trying to get through seminary and serve on the staff of the church. The pastor told me that this was the way it was supposed to be, and he told me how hard it had been for him to get through seminary and all about the demeaning jobs he had been required to endure. I wanted him to give me a raise or release me from some of my responsibilities, but instead he tried to one-up me in the sorrows department. His "help" just became one more sorrow in the end.

Of course, what he had to say was true, but it was not helpful except in one distinct way—my wife and I vowed never to do the same thing to others in the future. The truth is that there is usually little a mentor can do to alleviate the pain of this formative stage. The Great Physician prescribes the hardship of this struggle, and to take it away would be detrimental to the younger leader's growth. Nevertheless, although we may not be able to release people from their isolation, we can at least not make it all about us. We can offer prayers, heartfelt sympathy, and a shoulder to cry on. But even these are sometimes not in store for the leader during this phase; it is called "isolation" for a reason.

The type of intimacy learned at this stage of development can only be learned experientially. A Bible study cannot teach you what you need to learn. Even reading this book or another like it will not pass on to you the lessons that can be learned in the experience itself. The only solution is calling out to God and finding His presence to be the remedy for your loneliness. And you cannot find that solution without first being alone.

The good news is that for most of us this stage of development has an expiration date. It is a foundation for what is to come, and God intends the investment placed in you during these earlier phases to bear good fruit in the journeys to come.

In the case of Saul, he was about to ascend to a whole new level of significance. The next ten years of Saul's life would turn the world upside down, but they were built on the previous ten years of isolation and seeming fruitlessness. You cannot have world impact without first experiencing the personal impact of your earlier journeys. But that is not to say that at the end of isolation, all your lessons will have been learned. Many more are yet to be learned, on the foundations of those learned in struggle and isolation.

MATURING
IN MINISTRY
AND LIFE

PART TWO

The bathhouse in Perge. Paul and Barnabas preached the Gospel in this city at the end of the first journey.

The bathhouse in Perge.

3

The First Journey

"For This I Was Born"

It's what you learn after you know it all that really counts.
—John Wooden

He Himself gives to all people life and breath and all things;
and He made from one man every nation of mankind to live
on all the face of the earth, having determined their appointed
times and the boundaries of their habitation, that they
would seek God, if perhaps they might grope for Him and
find Him, though He is not far from each one of us; for in
Him we live and move and exist.
—the apostle Paul to the philosophers on Mars Hill (Acts 17:25–28)

RECENTLY I FOUND MYSELF ON A MISSIONARY JOURNEY—not from Antioch but to that city. The Lord had called several of us to visit Syrian Antioch in the fall of 2009 to hear from God concerning the way missions are done in the world today. Our modest hotel, directly in front of the ruins that once were the docks of Seleucia, stood between them and the ocean. The place where we spent the majority of our time would have been submerged when Barnabas and Saul set sail on their important mission. Two thousand years of silt runoff from the mountains above have pushed the sea's edge several hundred yards from the ancient docks, which now serve simply as a wall in a field where vegetables and spices are grown.

As the meetings went on, I often gazed out the window across the field at those large ancient stones and tried to imagine what Saul, Barnabas, and John Mark, the cousin of Barnabas (Colossians 4:10), must have looked like standing waiting there to board the ship that would take them

47

on a new journey. I pictured Barnabas sitting and looking very confident. I pictured his cousin seated beside him, less confident, watching Saul pace back and forth like a caged lion with his gaze on the horizon. How would it have felt to be about to embark on a trip without any idea of what to expect? No one had ever done before what they were about to do.

As far as we know, those three were the first missionary band ever commissioned by a church and sent to a foreign land.[1] Saul had been on many journeys before this one, but this was his real *first* missionary journey. I say this not simply because the heading in your Bible calls it that but because it was really the first of its kind. All his previous journeys—his trips to Jerusalem as a child, his travels to Damascus under orders as a persecutor, his return home to Tarsus as a dejected young man, his trip to Jerusalem from Antioch as a courier with a gift for famine relief—were small training operations for this day, his true first journey. Fifteen years after Saul's encounter with the Lord on the road to Damascus, God Himself finally said, "Go, now. This is what I have called you to. You're ready." The rest of history would refer to this as Paul's first missionary journey, but actually it was the first for us all.

Paul's Story: The First Journey

Around the spring of 47 A.D., Barnabas and Saul, along with John Mark, went down to the port in Seleucia and took a ship from there to Cyprus, which is where Barnabas was from. They landed in Salamis and began preaching in the synagogues there. John Mark is said to have been their helper or attendant. I assume that this didn't mean he carried their luggage for them, or that he functioned as some kind of roadie for the rock-star apostles. I imagine that it was more that he was to be an actual eyewitness of the things preached about Jesus. Eventually, this young helper would pen the Gospel of Mark. Perhaps as they traveled he rehearsed the story that he would eventually write down.

Although Cyprus was the home of Barnabas, he soon started to take a back seat to Saul's leadership. That may have been because of the problem we all experience—a prophet is not welcome in his hometown. It may also have been because Saul had stepped into a groove that all could recognize, and Barnabas was smart enough to ride the momentum. Given Barnabas's track record in Scripture, I favor the latter explanation. He truly lived to encourage and empower others in discovering their own purpose in God's redemptive mission.

No matter how much faith you have in the Gospel, when it actually works and souls are saved, it is always an amazing surprise. Even after all these centuries, the angels still rejoice at the phenomenon. I believe the apostles experienced the same pleasant surprise when they started preaching in Cyprus.

When they had gone from east to west through the island, they came to New Paphos, a city that was the capital of the island. There they came across a Jewish magician whom they considered a false prophet, and who went by the name Bar-Jesus, or Son of Jesus. This magician was an advisor of sorts to the Roman proconsul, Sergius Paulus, who was a very intelligent man. In his Pauline biography, John Pollock explains that Sergius Paulus had a scientific mind, which Pliny the Elder cited as an authority in his *Natural History.*[2] Sergius Paulus was curious and wanted to hear more from the apostles, and so he requested that they come and share their message with him.

In the counsel of the proconsul, however, was the magician Bar-Jesus. Clearly, the missionaries objected to this false prophet's being named Son of Jesus or Son of a Savior. In Acts, Luke calls him Elymas—perhaps a Semitic word for sorcerer, or possibly even his given name—rather than Son of Jesus. Saul goes further and twists it around and calls him "son of the devil."

In any case, the insecure sorcerer tried to dissuade the proconsul from hearing the message, probably because he was afraid of losing influence over such an important politician. Saul, full of the Holy Spirit, turned his attention to the disruptive influence and proclaimed, "You are full of all deceit and fraud, you son of the devil, you enemy of all righteousness, will you not cease to make crooked the straight ways of the Lord?" From Saul's charge, it seems clear that the sorcerer was attempting to counter what the apostles were telling Sergius Paulus. Saul was not done with him. He went on to say, "Now, behold, the hand of the Lord is upon you, and you will be blind and not see the sun for a time." With that, the false prophet went blind.

This was a plight that Saul himself was familiar with. It is appropriate that one so spiritually blind would suffer physical blindness as a judgment. It was temporary, as was Saul's.

We can only hope that Elymas found spiritual enlightenment as a result of his physical blindness, just as Saul had done. Luke describes the blindness as first being "a mist" over his sight, and then "a darkness." No one but Elymas himself could really know what the experience was like, and so there is a good chance that he later repented as a result and gave Luke his own recollection of the account. Of course this is conjecture, but not without some basis. In Luke's account, Saul does seem full of fury at the man, but we must remember Saul's experience of having gone blind by the hand of God and finding new enlightenment as a result. It is easy to think of Saul as callous and condemnatory at this moment. Personally, I can't help thinking that Saul was more sympathetic, since surely he would not have forgotten his own experience of blinding (Acts 9:9). Whatever happened with Elymas, one thing is certain—a door opened for the Gospel in the proconsul's court.

This moment seems to have been a turning point for the missionaries. From this point on, Saul was called Paul (his Roman name). It may simply be coincidence that Paul chose his Roman name over his Jewish name after meeting such a powerful leader who bore the same name. Perhaps he was reminded that his Roman name would be better received in a Gentile world. For whatever reason, from this point on he was known as Paul.

From here on, Paul apparently took the lead in the missionary work, and Barnabas seems to have taken a more supportive role. In fact, Luke goes so far as to refer to them as "Paul and his companions" at this point (Acts 13:13). Paul suddenly blossomed, as if he had been born for this work—and he had been (Galatians 1:15). Most leadership gifts are only truly discovered when the leader launches out into the world and tries them out to see how they fit. This role as an apostolic missionary fit Paul perfectly.

Sergius Paulus, hearing the message and seeing the powerful miracle of judgment against Elymas, believed in Christ.[3] This was a divine appointment that opened important doors for the missionaries and also revealed something about themselves.

After their experience in New Paphos, the team apparently went directly to the Galatian region of Asia Minor, without delay. Eckhard Schnabel suggests that Sergius Paulus may have given them important contacts in Antioch of Pisidia.[4] This may well be the case, since they seemed set on this course and did not stop or detour in spite of the long journey up a steep mountain, with the possibility of some sort of physical illness (Galatians 4:13–14). Once there, they began preaching the Gospel in the synagogues again.

When Jesus instructed the disciples in how to bring the Gospel of His kingdom to new people, He told them that they were to look for "a man of peace." If such a person were found, the missionary was to stay and focus on reaching all those connected to him (Luke 10:1–16). The pathways of the Gospel in the New Testament were relational connections called *oikos,* a word that our Bibles translate as "households," but it can have several meanings. It can mean more than a single family or house. It can be used to refer to a sort of network of close relational connections that would include slaves, one's intimate friends, and one's relatives.[5] All of Jesus' teaching on spreading the Gospel of His kingdom follows the tracks laid down from *oikos* to *oikos*.

This particular teaching of Jesus is expounded most fully in chapter ten of Luke's Gospel.[6] It follows that Luke would illustrate this teaching in real practice in his second volume—Acts. Luke has already demonstrated this powerful practice in earlier chapters and will do so again in later ones. Cornelius was a person of peace. He was asked to bring his *oikos* together to hear the good news. When he did, a large room full of his relatives and close friends all became followers (Acts 10:24). Some strategic basics will never change in ministry, and this relational approach is one of them. Jesus' teaching about reaching *oikos* after *oikos* through the person of peace is universal and still as relevant as ever.

In the second volume of his *Early Christian Mission*, Eckhard Schnabel establishes that there was a familial connection between Sergius Paulus and Sergii Paulii, who both owned estates in the region of Vetissus, which was in the province of Galatia, in central Anatolia.[7] It is entirely likely that once Sergius Paulus found the salvation of Jesus, he wanted others in his family to also hear this message of hope and thus set a path for the missionaries and opened some relational doors for the Gospel in this new territory. This likely explains the sudden directness with which the apostolic band headed up the steep incline to Antioch of Pisidia.

John Mark Heads Home

From New Paphos, the missionary band set sail for the Gulf of Attalia and then seven miles up the Cestrus River to Perga. Perga was a great city whose ruins are still a sight to see. At this point, John Mark chose to abandon the mission and return home. Luke does not say why.

Speculations for John Mark's departure are many. He may have been homesick. He may not have approved of Paul's rise in leadership over his older cousin Barnabas.[8] He may not have liked the concentration on Gentile *oikos* paths, or he may even have been aggrieved by such immersion in Gentile culture. This is unlikely, however, given that John Mark wrote his Gospel primarily with a Roman audience in mind. This variation in the journey may have represented a radical departure from the band's previous route. John Mark may have recognized the danger of exploring this particular region in the summer months, when malaria is a real threat, or he may have viewed the long uphill hike as too much to endure. The rigors of travel may have worn him down. He may have been suffering from culture shock. Or he may have had a more positive reason. Perhaps the way he was being used on this journey triggered a strong feeling that his Gospel account needed to be written as soon as possible. This last speculation, however, does not fit with Paul's adamant stance against taking John Mark on the second journey, and so a positive reason for his departure is less likely.[9]

On to Galatia

After John Mark left, Paul and Barnabas went on to Antioch of Pisidia.[10] Paul reminded the Galatian churches in this region that illness had caused him to bring the Gospel to them the first time (Galatians 4:13). Because of this reference, some speculate that Paul became sick with malaria and went to Pisidian Antioch, 3,600 feet above sea level, to seek relief there from the heat and the hungry mosquitoes. I find it more likely that he was following the relational *oikos* path that Sergius Paulus had given to him and Barnabas. The long hike up to Pisidian Antioch would have been very difficult for anyone who was ill, nor would Paul have been asked to speak in the synagogue in Pisidian Antioch if he had been so ill that he appeared sick. It is perhaps more likely that he became ill while in the Galatian region and so stayed there and thus was able to bring the Gospel to these people.

On the Sabbath, Paul and Barnabas found the synagogue and took their seats. As was customary, the visitors were invited to speak. Because Paul was a former Pharisee who had been mentored by Gamaliel, I imagine that the members of the synagogue must have been anxious to hear from him. And he certainly did not disappoint them—not that day. Paul rose from his seat and approached the table holding the scriptural scrolls. He greeted the people in customary fashion. But, against the tradition of the synagogues of the day, he also recognized the God-fearers in the crowd. Luke gives Paul's message a considerable number of lines to tell us that Paul preached to a primarily Jewish audience. Paul's message also harked back in many ways to Stephen's. It was as if Paul were continuing to fulfill the life he was partly responsible for cutting short.

All who heard the message seemed to be pleased. In fact, many surrounded Paul afterward, wanting to hear more and practically begging for him to return the following week. When he went to the synagogue the next Saturday, Luke says, "nearly the whole city assembled to hear the word of the Lord." This infuriated the regular members and made them jealous, and so Paul was not allowed to preach in the synagogue. But Paul rose anyway, without permission, and announced boldly: "It was necessary that the word of God be spoken to you first; since you repudiate it and judge yourselves unworthy of eternal life, behold, we are turning to the Gentiles. For the Lord has commanded us, 'I have placed you as a light for the Gentiles, that you may bring salvation to the end of the earth.' "

Paul and Barnabas then left the synagogue and probably went into the square and preached the word to a large crowd of receptive Gentiles and some Jews. In a rapid manner, Luke tells us, "the word of the Lord was being spread through the whole region." Like a virus of spiritual health, the reign of Christ spread in every direction. Perhaps part of their success was the fact that Paul and Barnabas were following up on the contacts given to them by Sergius Paulus.

Paul would follow this pattern during the rest of his journeys. He would preach the Gospel in a synagogue, if one could be found. In a short time the Jews would reject this new message, and a few would join Paul as he began preaching to the Gentiles, where he would see his greatest effectiveness. The Jews who rejected him would not leave him alone, though, but would stir controversy around him until finally persecution and beatings would chase him on to the next city. Antioch of Pisidia would be the first such city.

As Paul and Barnabas were chased out of town, they obeyed the Lord by shaking the dust off their feet in protest as they started off on the long road to the next town—Iconium. They stayed there preaching, to such an extent that the whole city seemed divided over their message. Some of the people threatened to mistreat them and stone them, and so they left. This pattern was repeated in Lycaonia, Lystra, and Derbe. Luke records some details of what occurred in those places.[11]

From Stardom to Stoning

While preaching in Lystra, Paul recognized that a man who had been lame his whole life had enough faith to be saved and healed. He stopped his message, gazed down at the man, and commanded him to rise and walk. The man jumped to his feet, healed.

The crowd was amazed at this miracle, so amazed that people in the crowd began speaking excitedly in the Lycaonian language, which Paul and Barnabas did not understand. As it turned out, the people thought that Paul and Barnabas were the fulfillment of a local legend concerning the god Zeus and his son and spokesman, Hermes.[12] According to the story, these Greek gods had come to this area in the form of mortal men, and the only ones to show them hospitality had been a couple named Philemon and Baucis. The gods punished all except this couple. The

Lycaonians, familiar with the story, saw this miracle and assumed that Barnabas was Zeus, and that Paul was Hermes because he was talking so much more. The local priest of Zeus, whose temple was just outside the city, brought oxen and garlands to the gates; he and the crowds wanted to offer sacrifice to them.

Once the apostles figured out what was going on, they tore their clothes, a traditional Jewish cultural expression for when one heard blasphemy. They ran out into the crowd to convince the people that they were just men, like all of them. It took some doing, but they managed to quiet the crowd just as some Jews from the previous town arrived, spotted the two, and convinced the crowd that Paul and Barnabas were not gods but charlatans.

In no time, Paul and Barnabas went from gods to goads, spurring a sharp reaction from the crowd, which turned quickly to a mob and then a gang of murderers. Some spontaneously picked up stones and began throwing them at Paul. Soon the whole crowd was throwing rocks at Paul, and he collapsed. The crowd grabbed his apparently lifeless body and dragged it out past the city boundary. Those who believed, along with a disheartened Barnabas, gathered around Paul's body, grieving and praying and perhaps planning a proper funeral. In this small gathering one might have seen Lois, Eunice, and a young teenager named Timothy, who were from this town (2 Timothy 3:10–11).

Did Paul, left for dead, actually die from the attack, and was he then resurrected? Some believe that this was the occasion when he went up to the third heaven, as recounted in 2 Corinthians 12. The timing is not right, however, for that event is said to have happened fourteen years before Paul wrote that epistle, which would put the event around 42 A.D., during Paul's dark days in Tarsus. Luke is careful not to say that Paul died in this exchange, and so perhaps we should join Luke in his caution. Had this been a legal execution, the authorities would have verified his death; as it was, however, the attackers were all in a hurry to leave the scene.

In the cool of the approaching evening, the small group gathered around Paul was surprised to see him rise, brush off what was left of the rocks and dust, and turn to walk back into town. Luke does not record that anyone said anything at this astonishing turn of events. He just goes on to tell us that the next day Paul and Barnabas left and journeyed thirty miles to Derbe. Near the end of his life, Paul would remind Timothy of the beatings he had witnessed Paul receiving in Antioch, Iconium, and Lystra (2 Timothy 3:10–11). Perhaps the incident with the confusion over the local tongue prompted the apostles to take Timothy along with them so that they had a "local" to help with the language and culture.

Timothy's being from a culturally mixed home (his father was Gentile and his mother Jewish), probably meant that he could speak more than one language and could also adapt well in cross-cultural settings. If so, this would have been the young lad's trial journey, with the thought that if he fared well they might call upon him in the future for even more work. Little did they all know how faithful this boy would come to be, and how Paul would adopt him as his own son (1 Corinthians 4:17; 1 Timothy 1:18; 2 Timothy 1:2, 2:1).

At some point close to this time, Paul became ill. Perhaps it was the stoning that left his body bruised, broken, and deformed and weakened his immunity. He remarks, writing to the churches of Galatia, "But you know that it was because of bodily illness that I preached the Gospel to you the first time; and that which was a trial to you in my bodily condition you did not despise or loathe, but you received me as an angel of God, as Christ Jesus Himself." Whatever the illness was, it affected his eyes. He goes on to say, "For I bear witness that, if possible, you would have plucked out your own eyes and given them to me" (Galatians 4:13–15). Perhaps his eyes were swollen—red as well as black and blue. But still he preached. He would later say to these people, "I bear on my body the brand-marks of Jesus" (Galatians 6:17).

The Long Way Home

Once Paul and Barnabas reached Derbe, they decided it was time to return home. From Derbe, it is not far over the mountains and land via Tarsus and then around the bay to Antioch. Their intention, however, was to return not merely to Antioch but to all the new churches. The apostles were feeling the burden of the lack of leadership in these new churches, and so they went back to each one to strengthen them all in any way they could, even though they faced the threat of further persecution. Luke says that they appointed elders in each church from among the new converts. The concern they felt must have been much like that of parents who know that hardship awaits their children and try to prepare them for what is to come.

From Antioch of Pisidia they ventured back down the pass into Pamphilia. This time they stopped in Perga to preach the Gospel. They then made their way to the harbor in Attalia and found a boat to Antioch. It is very possible that they met with catastrophe on this voyage home, for at some point between now and 56 A.D. Paul was shipwrecked three times, and this would have been his longest voyage in that time frame. But we are left with speculation, since Luke never tells us of these trials.

When they eventually arrived back at their home church, they celebrated by telling everyone about the wonders of their journey. Luke says that they spent a long time with the disciples there. It was during this time that Peter likely made a visit. He had freely sat at the table with the Gentiles and enjoyed fellowship—that is, until some legalistic leaders arrived from the Jerusalem church. These scrutinizing leaders, who claimed to have been sent by James, insisted that all who believed, including the Gentile converts, should follow Mosaic law. Their presence set the leaders in Antioch on edge. Most likely, in an attempt to keep peace among the brethren (and out of respect for James, the Lord's brother), Peter and some of the other Jewish leaders stopped dining with the Gentile believers. Paul points out that even Barnabas removed himself from the Gentile table. This infuriated Paul and may have been the first crack in their solid relationship, one that ultimately would lead to a permanent separation.

Some simply thought of this compromise as a way to keep the peace, but Paul saw it as a direct attack on the Gospel for which he had suffered and would ultimately die. In a public setting, he challenged Peter directly. He called him on his hypocrisy by asking him a straightforward question: If you are a Jew who lives like a Gentile, why now do you compel these Gentiles to live like Jews? Perhaps this type of rebuke reminded Peter of Jesus' rebuke for a similar hypocrisy, when he had denied his Lord. Peter must have responded well to this rebuke, however, because within a short time he would back Paul up in his conflicts with the Jerusalem church.

To solve the matter of what place Jewish law would play in the life of the new Gentile Christians, the Antioch church sent Paul and Barnabas to Jerusalem for council meetings with the leaders there. Even before they left for Jerusalem, Paul received word that the new churches in Galatia had fallen under deceptive teaching from Judaistic legalists who questioned Paul's authority as an apostle and his Gospel of grace. Before going to Jerusalem, Paul wrote a scathing letter to the new Christians in Galatia, rebuking them for abandoning the Gospel in favor of the law.[13] It was becoming apparent to the missionary, however, that it was problematic to make disciples and move on without first establishing on-site leadership. On his next journey, Paul would attempt a new strategy that was meant to avoid this problem.

When Paul and Barnabas went to Jerusalem, they told the elders their story of the great wonders that God had worked to verify the Gospel for these Gentiles. Peter was quick to add that he supported this new work, and he recounted his own example of how God had chosen him to bring the Gospel to the Gentiles. Finally James spoke up, quoting

Old Testament support and suggesting a solution that seemed to satisfy all present.

The meetings in Jerusalem were about more than the question of ritual practices. They were about even more than deciding whether Christianity would remain simply a sect of Judaism by making all the Gentile Christians become Jews. These meetings were truly about whether our souls are sanctified by God's grace or by our own works, and that is the single greatest battle of the New Testament. This was no less than a war over the Gospel itself. F. F. Bruce, in his outstanding commentary on Acts, says of this significant meeting: "The council of Jerusalem [was] an event to which Luke attache[d] the highest importance; it [was] as epoch-making, in his eyes, as the conversion of Paul or the preaching of the Gospel to Cornelius and his household."[14] Fortunately for all of us, the wisdom of these leaders and the Holy Spirit prevailed, with a decision that did not fracture the church or undermine the Gospel. In the end, it was settled that Gentile sanctification did not require the keeping of Mosaic law, which had been given to Israel. This allowed for two separate Christian lifestyles, Jewish and non-Jewish, something that would provide personal tension but also freedom to Paul in his ministry for the rest of his days.

Nevertheless, James's pronouncement and later teachings did not truly satisfy the legalistic Jewish Christians' point of view, and Paul would never be relieved of their constant hounding. But now Paul had a document directly from Peter, James the elder, and the Jerusalem church, verifying that the Gentiles did not need to become Jews in order to be Christians. Paul and Barnabas returned home, rejoicing in the good news.

Lessons of the First Journey

Paul and Barnabas's first journey was not only a first venture into cross-cultural overseas missionary activity on behalf of the church but also a great example of a new leader's first officially sanctioned ministry. And if we look carefully through the correct lenses, we can all see a bit of ourselves in this expedition.

The First Track Is Often the Fast Track

Paul and Barnabas covered 1,500 miles in one year, without any frequent flier miles. The first-journey leader tends to be hurried. As when a shaken bottle of champagne is opened, the release of the pressure built up in preparation for the mission tends to explode in a flurry of activity for the new leader.

It is quite common for a first-journey leader to see an early assignment as a stepping-stone to greater roles. This was not true of Paul, but the youth pastor pining for a senior role is common enough to be a cliché. I barely remember my twenties; they flew by fast because I was so anxious to grow up. What I do remember is being in a hurry to be more grown up and respected in others' eyes. In my last year of college, I used to head off to school carrying a briefcase, much to the chagrin of my wife, all because I wanted to appear more professional than a backpack would have made me look. Even the fact that I had married before my senior year was an indication of my fast track to becoming a grown-up.

I was a very serious person in my twenties and found that almost every decision was an important theological consideration. I was a self-appointed critic of others and prided myself on being a frontline scout of heresy in the church. Most of the people who know me today would be very surprised if they were to meet the twenty-five-year-old version of Neil Cole because so much has changed. For one thing, they would be shocked to see me in a full suit and tie every Sunday morning, which I wore by choice.

Lots of Activity

The first-journey leader's appetite for ministry is insatiable. Every opportunity to serve is swallowed whole. In my first pastorate, I was anxious to do everything in the church. I was excited to preach every sermon. I would welcome back any missionary and let him or her have "my" pulpit—for five minutes. But there was no way anyone was taking my preaching time. Later, I often wanted younger apprentice leaders to fill the pulpit while I listened and coached afterward. But that is not a first-journey characteristic. On my first journey, I was excited to conduct my first baptism, my first communion, and my first wedding. In fact, I was actually excited to do my first funeral, which sounds morbid and thought-less today.

The high level of activity during the first journey often produces a lot of ministry and even some fruitfulness. There were many churches started during Paul's first trip. Great future leaders, including Timothy, were the products of this journey. It is often the case that God works in spite of the first-journey leader, who may substitute lots of ministry activity for true intimacy with God.

I can certainly remember the good things that came of my ministry activity during my first journey, but one of the primary characteristics of all those good things is that they seem to have come about by accident.

The things I was trying to accomplish appeared to meet with failure, whereas other things just seemed to happen around me without much effort on my part. For example, my strategic outreach programs in the church yielded little or no fruit, but the paper route I took on to help make ends meet bore tremendous fruit.

First-journey leaders go after ministry rather than letting it come to them. They expend more energy in shorter bursts, with less fruit to show for their efforts in the end. This is why some of the greater fruit that comes at this stage of maturity appears to come about as if by accident rather than as the result of an intentional strategy.

I am convinced that God often saves us from our own ambitions during this phase because at these earlier stages of growth we do not have the perspective to really understand what success is. In my twenties, I was convinced that I needed to be the pastor of a megachurch in order to be successful. God had other plans, and far better ones, but I would not have had the maturity at this stage of life to be able to properly recognize that. Who knows, I might have even rejected God's plans if they had actually been shown to me at that time. I often wonder what I would be like now if God had granted all my ambitions from that time. This much is certain—I would not be the same person I am now.

This is not to take anything away from Paul and Barnabas's journey, but the exciting church-planting works of that journey resulted in weak and struggling churches. Timothy would wind up being a lasting and powerful gift to the kingdom of God, but during the first journey he may have been only an accidental footnote to the story (Luke does not even mention him on this journey). It is hard even to imagine Timothy's name coming up in the reports of their adventures that Barnabas and Paul delivered in Antioch and Jerusalem. Not until the second journey did Paul realize the potential of this young boy, but it was during even later journeys that this fruit came to be of monumental significance.

Identity Crisis

It is natural at this stage of development for the young leader to look to others with admiration and even a desire to emulate their success in ministry. The first-journey leader does not yet have the experience and maturity to realize fully who he or she is as a person or a leader. I remember many friends in seminary we referred to as MacArthurites because they tried so hard to look and sound like John MacArthur, who was quite popular in our area at that time. I also know a great many church planters who set out to emulate Rick Warren's or Bill Hybel's success and found out the hard way that mimicking someone else doesn't produce the same results.

First-journey leaders tend to believe that the results they are hoping for will depend on what they do, and so these leaders often engage in active imitation of the successful work of others. First-journey leaders are often looking for practical "how to's" at seminars and conferences. Any helpful practice that they can immediately employ to gain success is desirable. Eventually, if they progress in their development, they come to see the folly of this approach.

There was no *Church Planter's Toolkit,* or *Bootcamp* available to the first missionaries. They had little to draw on and methodically follow. It may be that Paul, from the sidelines, had observed the success of other ministries, such as the founding of the Antioch church, and emulated that success. Finally, though, his own turn came, and I imagine that he simply went about applying the same methods that others had used to find success. He may not have realized that on subsequent journeys he was going to learn much more than he ever could have learned from the people who had gone before him. The most important lessons of our lives do not come from books, seminars, or our mimicry of others but from our own hard lessons of failure and frustration.

Weaker Churches

Because first-journey leaders often try to do a ministry all by themselves, their churches may develop a dependency on these leaders. The result is that often first-journey leaders leave behind weakened churches.

The churches that were begun on Paul's first journey obviously didn't have strong leadership, partly because the apostles won converts and then left shortly thereafter. That's why Paul and Barnabas felt the need to go back and visit them again expressly to appoint leaders (Acts 14:23). Then they felt the need to visit them yet again (during the second journey) to strengthen them (Acts 15:36), even after Paul's stern letter (Acts 16:1–6). They were visited yet again a fourth time on Paul's third journey (Acts 18:23). These churches were not as self-sufficient as those that Paul began on later journeys. In fact, as I will attempt to demonstrate, Paul recognized the shortcomings of this first-journey strategy and made adjustments the second time around to compensate.

New leaders are drawn to do the work and do it well. It's good learning for them but often doesn't reproduce. The result is weaker churches that need special help from the outside to fill a leadership vacuum.

The Galatian churches were easily swayed by the leadership of the Judaizers who stepped in to fill the void after Paul's departure.

Emerging Influence

Apprentice leaders on the first journey become leaders in their own right, stepping out from the shadows of their mentors. Don't try to be someone you are not; become comfortable in your own skin. Even though first-journey leaders are not anywhere near the pinnacle of maturity in their ministries, they are still leaders who are serving the Lord, and they do produce results. People notice their gifts and their passion, and first-journey leaders will influence others, just not as much or as significantly as they will come to do on later journeys.

It is interesting to watch how Paul emerges as the true leader on this first trip. The journey begins with the Holy Spirit saying, "Set apart for me Barnabas and Saul for the work I have called them to." The team that leaves is referred to as Barnabas and Saul (Acts 13:7), but as the journey progresses the terminology is transposed to "Paul and Barnabas" (Acts 13:42, 43, 46). As already mentioned, at one point the team is referred to as "Paul and his companions" (Acts 13:13), and Barnabas is left out altogether.

Barnabas was a bit further down the maturity track than Paul. We simply must admire his humility, as demonstrated by his encouraging Paul to lead. The "son of encouragement," as he was called, was always looking to make others around him successful, and with Paul he succeeded. Apparently he also succeeded with John Mark, since Paul would later comment repeatedly on John Mark's effectiveness in missionary work even though he refused his service on the second trip (Colossians 4:10; Philemon 24; 2 Timothy 4:11).

A Necessary Journey

The first journey is probably the least effective journey of a leader's life, but it is necessary. On the first journey, the leader gains practical know-how that later will be passed on to others. For this reason, no one can skip the first journey. It will bear fruit that lasts, one hopes, but one also hopes that it will not be the most productive period of a leader's life.

Each of life's journeys has its own progression. The leader Paul was when he embarked from the harbor in Seleucia was not the same leader who returned a year later. In the next chapter, we will discover that the lessons Paul learned on his first journey bore significant consequences for his second.

As I progressed on my own first journey, I began to recognize some of the weaknesses of what I had been doing, and I made some changes. This is probably what is most necessary in order for a leader to move on to the second journey.

I do not remember when it happened, but at some point the suits and ties were relegated to collecting dust in my closet, the briefcase was replaced with a backpack, and I was more comfortable being the man God had made me to be than striving to be the next MacArthur, Hybels, or Warren. I settled into the realization that having a megachurch might not be the greatest pursuit of my life, and I discovered other ambitions that were more suited to my own gifts and calling. I am so grateful that God delivered me from my younger ambitions!

Another thing that happened during the later part of my first journey was that I became very content with the church I was leading. In fact, I more or less lost the desire to move on to something else. It was actually when I had stopped looking for something else that God moved me on, and I went—almost reluctantly.

I distinctly remember that turning thirty was a shock. I realized that I had sped through my twenties and would never get those years back. I didn't regret them, but I determined to enjoy my thirties much more.

A memorable moment came at the end of my first journey, when I was to meet with Bob Logan and Steve Ogne to discuss a possible ministry move. Bob and Steve had published several church-planting resources, and I was excited that they were showing an interest in me. What was most memorable about this meeting is that our family car was not available to me on that day, and so I rode my newly acquired skateboard to the meeting. I had bought the skateboard at a garage sale because in my serious first-journey years I had missed having fun. As a kid, I really had enjoyed skateboarding.

I didn't care if Bob or Steve thought it was immature. I didn't even stop to question it. Frankly, I told myself, if they didn't like me for who I was, then I didn't want to work with them. The meeting was only about a mile from my home, and without a car, I simply took up the skateboard and went off to this important meeting without any concerns. It turned out that they were quite amused by it, and we worked together on some fairly significant projects that later evolved into our understanding of the organic nature of the church.

I have had a lot more fun in my thirties and forties than I did in my twenties. I don't miss the person I was back then, but I must confess—I wish I still had the same body I did then. It is said that youth is wasted on the young. I understand that.

Other than to the occasional funeral or wedding, I haven't worn a suit and tie in about twenty years. I still prefer a backpack to a briefcase. I found on my later journeys that there were problems with my riding a skateboard, so I passed mine along to my son. My son still has that skateboard.

The Roman docks in Corinth from which Paul set sail at the end of his second journey.

4

The Second Journey
Learning Can Be a Pain

If you want to make God laugh, tell him your plans.
—Woody Allen

For to me, to live is Christ and to die is gain.
—the apostle Paul (Philippians 1:21)

THERE IS A SECOND-CENTURY document that was widely respected by the early church called Acts of Paul and Thecla. It contains a description of the apostle Paul on his first journey that may be a retelling of a traditional story from the Iconium region. In the only physical picture we have of the apostle, Paul is described as short and balding, with a large hooked nose and bushy eyebrows that meet above it. It says that he walked with crooked legs, perhaps from the beatings he'd received, but nevertheless with the strength of a fit body from having walked thousands of miles.

It was not Paul's external appearance that drew people to him. It was the light in his soul, as shown in the rest of the description, which says that he had a face full of friendliness, with a big inviting smile that lit up for all he greeted. His face is said to have seemed at times like the face of an angel.[1] Paul may have had the face of an angel at times, but if you crossed him and threatened his Gospel, I imagine you would not have wanted to be facing that hooked nose topped by a furrowed unibrow!

Paul's first journey, with all its hardships, presented so much success that it is hard to imagine Paul trying to fix any part of his strategy. Success can be seductive, however. It leaves us satisfied but at the same time strangely insecure. In any case, success should not really be our primary objective, because it is short-lived and can be deceptive. It sometimes takes conflict, confusion, frustration, pain, failure, loneliness, and fear to break us out of that seduction so that we can learn the lessons that go beyond our initial success. That is what the second journey provided for Paul. It was full of great highs, found at the end of very deep and dark valleys, where the true lessons are learned best. And these are the lessons that lead to mountaintop experiences.

Paul's Story: The Second Journey

After the obvious success of the first journey, it would have been natural for Paul to expect his second to be the same. Perhaps it might have been if a disagreement had not intervened.

Paul Flies Out on Wings All His Own

Acts tells us that Paul proposed to Barnabas that they visit all the cities where they had proclaimed the word of the Lord. These two spiritual parents were worried about the welfare of their new Galatian churches. Had the churches received the letter Paul had sent them? Had they responded well to its message?[2] Now that they had the official letter from James and the Jerusalem church council, they were anxious to bring the good news to the churches and, hopefully, settle some of the conflict. As plans were being made, a sharp disagreement arose between Paul and Barnabas over who should go. At least that was the pretext for the heated argument. There may very likely have been other issues brewing under the surface.

Most likely because he believed that past behavior is the best predictor of future behavior, Paul did not want John Mark, who had deserted them on the first journey, to accompany him and Barnabas. Barnabas was of the persuasion that people could change and needed to be given the chance to grow and develop. I'm sure he was not shy about using Paul's own story as evidence for his point of view. Their disagreement was so serious that they parted ways. John Mark was the ostensible reason for the breakup, but there were other cracks in the foundation of their partnership.

We can speculate on other possible causes for the division, and they are not hard to discern. Paul was undoubtedly disappointed in Barnabas for choosing to dine exclusively with the Jews when the representatives from Jerusalem came (Galatians 2:13). Paul also had grown in his leadership gifts on that first journey and now was ready to set the agenda from the very start. Perhaps Paul wished that his partner were also a Roman citizen so that they could escape some of the beatings he had had to endure. But Barnabas was not a Roman citizen, and Paul would never have abandoned his teammate in the heat of the battle.

There is a chance that Barnabas felt disrespected by the apprentice to whom he had given much humble support and opportunity. He may even have harbored some disdain for the way Paul had taken things over, although his track record does not merit this speculation. Perhaps more than anything, Barnabas seems to have been wired to see the potential in others and to have been particularly gifted at drawing that potential out. He did so with Paul and also with John Mark (Colossians 4:10; 2 Timothy 4:11). He could no sooner deny this impulse than deny the Spirit of God in him. Paul may have been great at preaching the Gospel and forming new churches, but Barnabas's gift was equally valuable. To deny it would have been to deny the gifts and the leading of Jesus. Barnabas was as adamant about following God's lead regarding his assessment of people's hearts as Paul was about defending his Gospel. Neither would have backed down, and so a split was inevitable.

Barnabas took John Mark and headed back to Cyprus. Paul called Silas back from Jerusalem, and together they took the land route toward the Galatian region. Silas was a good choice for Paul because he could represent the Jerusalem church as they took the letter from James abroad. Silas, like Paul, was also a Roman citizen (Acts 16:37), which may have been helpful when they faced the inevitable persecution.

Whatever the reason for the breakup, it was not all bad. Now there were two teams covering twice as much ground and starting twice as many churches. Providentially, this was a lesson of the second journey, but it would not truly be realized until deeper pain made it more obvious. God was the master teacher, and He had an important lesson for Paul, but this was only the start. When God has something important to teach us, pain is often the vehicle that gets us to recognize and remember the truth. This is true for all of us, and it was true for Paul as well.

On this trip, Paul took the lead from the start. He chose the team, the route, and the strategy. And he would improve upon the previous work by doing things better. The Galatian churches were weak and vulnerable to domineering leadership. They had become victims of bigoted and bullying legalists, and he would find a strategic way of preventing that from happening again.

The first part of Paul's adjusted strategy was to recruit a larger team. Over the course of traveling from Antioch through southern Galatia, past Mysia and all the way to the coastal city of Troas, he recruited Timothy and Luke, which made this team twice the size of the original missionary team.[3]

Young Timothy, probably around twenty-one years old at this time, had already demonstrated strong leadership gifts and a heart for the Lord. But to join in on this next journey, he had to count the cost. Timothy had a Jewish mother, which by canonical law made him a Jew even though his deceased father was Greek. His father had objected to circumcision because he saw it as cruel or because he wanted to prevent embarrassment for his boy in the gymnasium, or because of both reasons. Timothy, having lost his father and been raised by his mother and his grandmother, was likely yearning for a father figure in his life (Philippians 2:22), and Paul showed great interest in him. The one hitch in the arrangement was that Paul's strategy made visiting the synagogue crucial to the mission, and Timothy would have been considered an unwelcome apostate Jew unless he had been circumcised. In a move that must have seemed quite contrary to the mission of spreading news of the Jerusalem council's decision concerning the Gentiles, especially in light of the letter he had just written to the Galatian churches (Galatians 5:1–6, 6:12–16), Paul stepped into the role of Timothy's father (1 Timothy 1:2; 2 Timothy 1:2) and circumcised him. Because Timothy was Jewish, this was a simple act of obedience to the Old Testament law, and it was not a violation of Paul's own belief that those who were Gentiles did not need to become Jews in order to be followers of Christ. Not only did this move fully restore Timothy to the nation of Israel, it also granted him access to the synagogues during the missionary journeys, and so this act was very helpful.

Timothy became a member of the missionary band and remained a faithful son to Paul all the rest of their days (Philippians 2:22). I sometimes chuckle at the words of Paul to Timothy, reminding him of the suffering he had had to endure to bring the Gospel to Timothy's people (2 Timothy 3:10–12), all the while knowing the suffering that Timothy had had to go through to bring the Gospel to Paul's! At any rate, this young man proved early on that he was willing to count the cost and remain faithful, and that quality would always characterize his life (Philippians 2:19–23). He passed Paul's test of what made a strong church planter, whereas John Mark had not, at least not at this moment in the story.

Plan A Rejected

Until this point, Paul was pretty sure of what they were going to do. He was drawn to the great potential of the most influential city in all of Asia—Ephesus. The "A" in plan A stood for *Asia Minor*. Luke tells us, however, that the Holy Spirit forbade them from speaking the word in Asia.

We are not told the details of how this leading came to the team. Silas was a mature and experienced prophet, and so it is possible that it came through him. Apostles and prophets worked well together in pioneering the church, as the prophetic role provided spiritual intelligence that informed apostolic action. This could well have been the case with these two. Paul was often given direction from the Lord, and so it wasn't necessary for it to come through Silas. It could have been geopolitical or legal circumstances that prevented them. We do not know how God got the message across, but an even more compelling question is *Why?*

Certainly Paul's view of the strategic influence of Ephesus and Asia Minor was sound, as would prove true later on. The prohibition against Asia was only temporary. It was not that God didn't like Asians; in fact, it is clear that God had great plans for Asia. It may well have been that the soil in Asia was just not quite ready for Paul's message, but I hold a different viewpoint. I believe that Paul himself was not ready for the work God had planned in Asia. There was a great work waiting in Asia but also a great adversary, and Paul had some lessons to learn before he would be ready for this adventure. Therefore, the second journey would have to take him down another path. I will expand more on the adversary that Paul would ultimately meet in Asia when I look more closely at his third journey.

The prohibition was not to stay out of Asia but not to speak the word there. Ouch! That is, in many ways, worse. They really couldn't avoid traveling through Asia Minor, but they were clearly forbidden by the Holy Spirit to speak the word there. From all that we know of Paul, this must have been the hardest lesson of obedience yet—to have gone all that way, sent by the Antioch fellowship, with documents endorsing their mission from the Jerusalem leadership, only to have the highest authority in the universe forbid any evangelism. This must have gravely disappointed and frustrated Paul. I can imagine that he was not easy to live with at that moment, and young Timothy may have been asking the question, "What have I done?"

Plan B Also Rejected

Paul, like any other good leader whose plan A has been shut down, quickly rallied his team to plan B, where the "B" stood for Bithynia, to the north. They made their way to Mysia, where they intended to make entry into this influential northern region.[4]

As Acts says, the Spirit of Jesus did not permit them to reach Bithynia, either. They had been prohibited from preaching during their travels through Asia, and now the Spirit of Jesus let them know that they were not to enter the land to the north.

Therefore, they were unable either to go south or venture north. The missionaries would never have retreated to the regions already reached in the east, and so they could only go forward, toward the coast. Paul, no doubt feeling like a missionary pinball bouncing from one prohibition to another, and forbidden to preach the message that burned in his heart, must have been at wit's end when they landed on the coast in Troas. The Holy Spirit had led them to this place, where they completed the team by acquiring Luke.[5]

Now, with no plan but with a complete team, and with the seemingly endless horizon of the sea before them, Paul and the others were primed to finally hear God's plan. God's ways are unpredictable. Your master plan is always second to your Master's plan! No matter how much we think we have it figured out, in the end we can only wave the white flag and surrender to God's plan if we hope to accomplish anything good. That message alone was worth the long voyage to Troas. In the literal dark of night, and in the metaphorical darkness of not knowing what God wanted, Paul finally saw God's plan revealed: plan M, where "M" stood for Macedonia. Luke says that a vision came to Paul: "A man of Macedonia was standing and appealing to him, and saying, 'Come over to Macedonia and help us.'"

Imagine the relief they felt when they finally got this direction. They immediately found passage on a ship heading past Samothrace to Neapolis. From darkness to direction, they now knew what they were to do, and everything seemed to fall into place. The frustration and confusion were behind them—and so was a strong wind. In only two days, they made it to their destination, a trip that would take them more than twice as long on the way back (Acts 20:6). Following the Lord's direction is always much easier than trying to force your own plans—not that the rest of Paul's journey was going to be easy. There was still much for Paul to learn in preparation for the other journeys he would take.

The First Disciples in Europe (Philippi)

They walked up to Philippi from Neapolis. Philippi, a leading city of eastern Macedonia named after Alexander the Great's father, Phillip, was a Roman colony—a little Rome. It was full of Roman pride, Latin was spoken in all official business, and Roman citizenship was held in very high regard. It was also a strategic military post, and so it was full of soldiers both active and retired. It was near this place that Marc Antony and Octavian (later the Emperor Augustus) defeated the traitors Brutus and Cassius, who had assassinated Julius Caesar on the senate floor. This place was very pro-Rome in every way.

Luke says that they stayed there many days. Normally, Paul would enter the synagogue and preach the Gospel. Once some had come to believe, he would move on to the next city. But in Philippi, he did things differently. First of all, there was no synagogue, which meant that there were not even ten Jewish men in the whole city.

Paul, having grown up in a Jewish community in Tarsus, intuitively knew how to scope out the Jews living in the midst of Gentile cities even when there was not a synagogue (Acts 16:12–13). His pattern was always first to preach the Gospel to the Jews who were living in foreign cities. This was a group he could relate to on many levels; they were, in a sense, his people, although usually they would not accept him as such. Like Jesus, he went to his own, and his own did not accept him.

On the first Sabbath, the missionaries went past the northwestern gate, built in honor of Augustus, and walked about a mile and a half along a shaded road down to the Gangites River, hoping to find a place of prayer. There they found a group of God-fearers (Gentiles who believed in Judaism but were not yet proselytes or circumcised) who listened to their message. A prominent Asian businesswoman, Lydia from Thyatira, was a seller of purple fabrics who "opened her heart to respond to the things spoken by Paul."

Lydia and all of her *oikos* (household) were baptized. She would not accept no for an answer when she invited them to stay at her home while they were in town. Her house became the outpost for the Philippian mission.

Paul's normal pattern, whether he was chased out by persecution or not, was to leave the church in the care of the Holy Spirit and move on to the next town (Acts 13:5–6, 12–14; Acts 14:25; Acts 17:33–18:1), but this time he didn't. The apostles continued walking the streets of Philippi as if looking for someone.

In every city of the world there are evil men who get wealthy at the expense of young women, and Philippi was no different. In this case, a demonized slave girl was being exploited for a fortune-telling business that was owned by some kind of syndicate. A strange voice completely beyond her control would come out of her body and predict the future. We can assume that the crafty demons would then arrange circumstances to "fulfill" the predictions, thus preying on the fearful and superstitious nature of the people.

As Paul and Silas roamed the streets, she would follow them and occasionally shout out in a demonic voice, "These men are bond servants of the Most High God, who are proclaiming to you the way of salvation." At first Paul just ignored her and went about his business. But her following and shouting at Paul and Silas raised much concern and curiosity among the Philippians, who would have highly respected her spiritual insights as coming from a god. Paul wanted no part of free demonic publicity or of people exploiting her bondage, and so he turned and, with authority, cast the demons out of her and set her free.

The syndicate that had been exploiting her was outraged at the loss of its business. Paul and Silas were dragged before the magistrates and accused of trying to get the good Roman citizens of Philippi to disobey the laws of Rome. It was also noted that they were Jews. Just before this time, a law had been passed to banish all Jews from Rome, and so in a place like Philippi, which had no Jews and was a proud Roman colony, this was enough to get the apostles publicly beaten with rods and tossed into jail without a fair trial.

But there was something wrong with this picture. Paul and Silas were both officially Roman citizens, which would have prevented their being beaten and jailed. Why did Paul not mention their status? It couldn't be that they forgot about it. How many blows would you need across your back before remembering that you had a "get out of beating free" card? No, they understood well the circumstances and the climate and could easily have flashed their credentials if they had wanted to. We know this because they did show them the next day, after the beating. In Philippi, Roman citizenship was very valued and respected (Philippians 3:20–21).[6] So why did they endure a beating when they didn't need to? I believe it was for the same reason that they were still in Philippi and had not moved on. They were looking for someone and wouldn't rest until they found him. They had to endure this beating in order to find the path that would lead them to him.

Luke's writing style is always quite precise, but in Acts 16:19–20 he makes a statement that appears to be redundant. It is so out of character that the scholar William Ramsay speculates that Luke never actually finished the manuscript as he would have liked.[7] But we need not doubt the veracity of the Scripture here. Instead we can ask why Luke would have used two different but almost identical terms to describe who was sentencing them.

One of the terms used was a common Greek expression, but the other term was a more official Roman title for roughly the same type of officer. It may be that the court that first assembled was merely a local band of officials and that the Roman representatives, including the Roman jailer, then appeared and presided. If indeed Luke's language is precise, he must have intended us to ask why he had used both terms, and I believe that this is the best answer and is a clue for us to discover why the missionaries kept silent about their Roman citizenship.[8]

The jailer locked their feet in shackles in the deepest part of the jail. Unable to sleep because of the pain, the two began to pray and sing praises to the Lord. I imagine the hopeful voices of these undefeated apostles combined with the acoustics of the solid stone walls, ceilings, and floors to make for quite a beautiful and soulful worship experience. Perhaps Silas was also speaking prophetic words over some of the men in prison or even gave a prophecy of the impending earthquake. For whatever reason, those in the prison were so amazed by these two prisoners' sense of peace and freedom that they felt compelled to stay, even when a chance for freedom presented itself.

About midnight, when the earthquake hit, the chains fell off all the prisoners' wrists and ankles, and the doors swung open. The earthquake awakened the jailer, who grabbed his sword and rushed downstairs to check on his charges. What he had feared the most lay before him—the doors were wide open, and there was only darkness inside. As a military man, he knew that the only noble recourse for his failure was suicide. He drew his small blade from its sheath and was about to plunge it into his heart when he heard a voice.

I imagine that Paul, inside the jail and looking out through the doorway, saw in the moonlight the silhouette of a figure drawing his blade. Paul called out, "Do not harm yourself, for we are all here!" The jailer, in frantic hope and nagging unbelief, called for lights from his slaves and found that Paul's words were true—all the prisoners had stayed. They had found greater freedom with Paul and Silas in the Gospel than they would have found in an escape from the jail. The seasoned battle veteran with the sword came trembling in fear before the apostles, dropped to his knees, and asked, "Sirs, what must I do to be saved?"

What would cause such a response? There was much at work in this scenario. God had arranged the whole thing, and Paul and Silas knew it. The fortune-teller had already spread their reputation as being from the highest God and having the way of salvation. The joyful and unquenchable spirits of Paul and Silas, as they sang in the face of physical pain, were a strong draw for those who were in that jail. The localized and unusual earthquake would have made the superstitious people think that the Most High God was not pleased with how his bond servants were being treated. All of this was what had caused their fellow inmates and their keeper to react in such a highly unusual manner. Fear of the Most High God had come upon them, and they did not choose the alternative of escape, whether by running or by suicide.

Paul responded to the jailer's request by saying, "Believe in the Lord Jesus, and you will be saved, you and your household [*oikos*]." I used to think that Paul was being prophetic when he announced the salvation of the jailer's entire household, but lately I have come to see this another way. Paul was not speaking prophetically but strategically and confidently, on the basis of previous revelations. The jailer was not just a man of peace whose household would now come to Jesus, although he was that. He may have actually been the man of whom Paul had a vision in Troas, a Macedonian who called out to Paul. "Come over here and help *us*" (emphasis added). I believe that this was the man Paul and Silas had been searching for all along, and that he is the reason they remained in Philippi even after a viable church had been started. That would explain why they endured the seemingly unnecessary pain of being beaten with rods.[9] Paul had traveled hundreds of miles over land and sea to find this man, and he wouldn't have let a whipping stop him from accomplishing his mission.

There was much rejoicing. The jailer washed their wounds, and Paul and Silas symbolically washed away the jailer's sins in baptism, along with those of his entire household—his wife, his children, his slaves and workers—and perhaps even those of some of the inmates.

In the morning, word came from the magistrates to let the Jewish prisoners go. The jailer was overjoyed to deliver that message but shocked when he heard Paul's response. It was at this time that Paul let them know of his and Silas's Roman citizenship. When the officials heard that the men they had beaten in public and locked in prison were Roman citizens, they became afraid. Their exalted view of Rome suddenly was turned against them. They came to the beaten Roman citizens and begged them to leave town.

The Shortcomings in Paul's New Strategy

After they visited once more with the church in Lydia's home, Paul and his companions obliged and left town. Perhaps they were hoping that the fear the city officials felt was enough to secure peace for the new churches in their absence. But that wasn't all Paul wanted to do for the church in his absence. Here we see another change in his previous missionary pattern. Luke stayed behind in Philippi. This is a clue to another shift in Paul's strategy from the first journey. I believe that Paul recruited a larger team in order to leave workers behind to nurture the young churches through the vulnerable early days without slowing down the progress of the missionary journey. He did so to adjust the previous strategy, which had left behind "orphaned" churches that had no leadership in their impressionable first days.

Paul, Silas, and Timothy traveled from Philippi through Amphipolis and Apollonia until they arrived at Thessalonica. There they found a synagogue and stayed three weeks, reasoning from the Scriptures with the Jews about the evidence of Jesus being the Messiah.

Eventually some God-fearers and Gentiles, along with a few Jews, came to believe, and a church was born. Once again strife followed, and it came to a head when a mob pursued Paul and Silas for turning their world upside down. After the crowd calmed down, the new believers sent the missionaries away by night. Timothy stayed behind, in accord with Paul's newer strategy.[10]

When they arrived in Berea, Paul and Silas found the Jews there more receptive, but the angry Thessalonians were not content with having the apostles move on. They came after them to Berea to cause trouble. Many of the people in Berea believed, but the crowds were stirred up once again, and so it was impossible for Paul to stay. A few of the local believers took him farther south, all the way to Athens, and Silas was left behind with the new church in Berea, just as Luke had stayed in Philippi and Timothy had remained in Thessalonica. Paul was now without his team. Some plans look good on paper, but in real life they quickly fall apart.

After Paul arrived in Athens and his escort went back to Berea, he realized that his new strategy was shortsighted. He was alone. He would never be able to recruit a team large enough to leave leaders behind at each stop.

This may all seem perfectly obvious to us, looking back two thousand years. The reality, however, is that most of us resort to recruiting leaders to fill ministry needs in much the same way, and our own strategies meet the same dead-end results. Whenever we resort to recruiting leaders, we find that there is more of a need for ministry than there are leaders to fill it. We should keep this in mind before we conclude that Paul was foolish for attempting what we have all done so often. In fact, that is one of the reasons why I wrote this book—so we can learn from the same lessons that Jesus taught Paul.

Lonely Journeys to Athens and Corinth

It was very hard for Paul to be alone once again after his years in Tarsus. He didn't do well alone and usually avoided solitude. Even in solitary confinement while on death row in Rome he said, "Luke is with me" (2 Timothy 4:11). Talk about a faithful companion! There are not many who get to have a friend with them in the dungeon, nor are there many friends who would oblige. At this juncture, at the end of his strategy on this second journey, Paul found himself alone in a foreign city full of demonic idols. Luke says that he was "provoked" by the idolatry he witnessed. He was motivated to speak the word of God and try to reason with the people.

Athens at this time was long past her glory days as the global center of cultural and philosophical advancement. Luke comments that the people, perhaps still longing for the good old days, had nothing better to do with their time "than telling or hearing something new." Paul was glad to oblige by reasoning every day with the people in the synagogue and the marketplace. The Epicurean and Stoic philosophers wanted to hear more, and so they invited him to preach at the Areopagus. The Areopagus, sometimes called Mars Hill, was a large rock where court was held. It was here that Socrates met his accusers, but by the time Paul was taken to this historic site, much of the authority of the court had been diminished, and so at that time they evaluated issues of education and general matters related to the marketplace.[11]

When Paul spoke to the philosophers on Mars Hill, he presented a masterful sermon—short and to the point, with illustrations from his audience's common experience as well as quotes from some of their own prized literature. It is amazing that this man, the author of the poem of true love in 1 Corinthians 13 (read around the world at weddings), said of himself, "I did not come in superiority of speech or of wisdom." This sermon demonstrates that he was indeed a man of great oratory abilities when empowered by the Holy Spirit and speaking about what he loved most in life.

After his brief message, some believed, but most did not. Paul did not stay. Perhaps he was so provoked by the city's idolatry, a provocation accentuated by his own sense of loneliness, that he left a new church behind and went to Corinth.

In many respects, Corinth was the sin capital of the world. It had a quarter of a million people jammed into a relatively small place and was the largest city (apart from Antioch) that Paul had encountered on his missionary journeys so far. It sat on an isthmus, a narrow bridge of land connecting the much larger landmasses of Macedonia and Achaia. As a result, Corinth was a crossroads from every direction, by land and by sea, with two ports, one on each side. People using the shipping routes found it more economical to sail into the port on one side of Corinth, unload their cargo, transport it across the four-mile isthmus, and reload it on another ship than to sail the two hundred treacherous miles around the many capes of the Pelopponeus, the large landmass of Achaia. They would even put their smaller ships on rollers and tow them across the land and relaunch them on the other side.

Try to imagine what the city must have looked like when all the sailors and their cargo, legal and illegal, got off at one place. To add to this environment, Corinth was most famous for its temple to the goddess Aphrodite, on top of its acropolis. This cult was dedicated to glorifying sex, with a thousand temple prostitutes devoted to that mission. The phrase *act the Corinthian* became synonymous with committing fornication, and *Corinthian girl* was a term for a harlot.

Paul, alone in a sea of people and sin, was afraid. The idolatry in Athens provoked him, but the wanton sinfulness of Corinth had a different affect—he was frightened. It is hard for us who read the New Testament, with all his exploits, ever to think that the great apostle Paul was afraid of anything, but he was. Later he said to the Corinthians, "I was with you in weakness and in fear and in much trembling" (1 Corinthians 2:3). Lest you consider this hyperbole from a humble apostle, there is one other witness to verify his fear. At night, while Paul was alone and afraid, Jesus came to him in a vision and said, "Do not be afraid any longer, but go on speaking and do not be silent; for I am with you, and no man will attack you in order to harm you, for I have many people in this city" (Acts 18:9–10).

These words from Jesus were not simply comforting words to strengthen Paul's resolve in the face of his fears. There was a strategic lesson in these words that would alter his missionary endeavors in permanent and powerful ways.

Until this moment Paul's strategy had been to go to a town, win as many disciples as possible, starting with the Jews, and then move on to the next town or city to do it all again. On this second journey, having seen the weakness of the Galatian churches, he altered his strategy by recruiting more leaders and leaving them behind to oversee the young churches while he moved on to the next town. Here, at the end of his rope, he realized the futility of his new strategy. It was when Paul was in this weak and broken state that Jesus finally stepped in to give him a new strategy, one that would eventually reach the entire Gentile world and change history.

Jesus' Plan

In essence, Jesus instructed Paul not to leave so quickly. Rather than recruiting and importing a team of leaders, he is to find them in the harvest fields. To his fear Jesus said, "Do not be afraid." To his pain Jesus said, "No man will attack you to hurt you." To his loneliness Jesus said, "I am with you." To his shortsighted strategy Jesus said, "Do not be silent, but go on speaking, for I have many people in this place." In other words, find your team here among these sinful people; don't wait for Silas and Timothy to come.

I believe that it was at this time that Paul sought to find a place to ply his trade.[12] After hearing from Jesus, Paul changed his approach to mission and stayed in Corinth, which was a good place to be a tent maker. With its large population, its bustling marketplaces, and its location at times as the site of the Isthmian games, it needed tents.[13]

In his vocation, Paul met Aquila and Priscilla, who had been forced out of Rome because they were Jewish. Paul had much in common with this couple, and so he joined them in trade and living. Luke then tells us that Paul set out to reason daily in the synagogues with the Jews. Aquila and Pricilla accompanied him and came to be persuaded to follow Jesus.[14] Paul found new team members who would work with him throughout his life, right where Jesus said he would—in this sinful place. Aquila and Priscilla were only the start; there would be many more, including Cripus, the leader of the synagogue, and the well-respected Titius Gaius, who hosted the new church in his spacious home next door to the synagogue. Even the wealthy city treasurer, Erastus, would become part of the church (Romans 16:23).[15]

Acts tells us that Paul stayed a year and a half in Corinth after he heard from Jesus, a clear indication of a dramatic change in his strategic approach to the mission. A year and half is a long time to stay in one place for a man who had traveled 1,500 miles in one year on his previous journey. Paul's methods would shift from an addition strategy to one of multiplication. He would no longer just add disciples to the church but would raise leaders from the harvest in order to multiply the influence of Christ's word over entire regions and ultimately over the Roman Empire.

After his work was done in Corinth and threats began to mount against him, Paul did the sensible thing—he stayed longer. I believe that in part this was not because the work needed him but because Jesus told him personally that no harm would come to him there. Paul chose to put his faith in Jesus' words and prove them true instead of letting the circumstances around him dictate his agenda. Fear was no longer an issue. Jesus took care of that and much more. Of course, Jesus' words were faithful and true.

The Return Trip

After enough time had passed to prove his point, Paul set sail for Syria, accompanied by Aquila and Priscilla. When they reached Ephesus, Paul went to the synagogue and reasoned with the Jews, but only for a little while. As soon as he saw that they were receptive and wanted him to stay longer, he left. Why? I believe he wanted to test whether the prohibition against preaching in Asia had been lifted after he learned the lessons of the second journey. The Holy Spirit had forbidden him to preach the Gospel in Asia, but not to Asians (Lydia in Philippi was from Thyatira, a city in Asia Minor). It appears that the prohibition had been lifted, and so he was hoping to return but not planning for it. He had learned well, and so he said, "I will return to you again *if God wills*" (emphasis added).[16] It appears that he just dipped his toes in the water of Asia to see if it was safe to jump in, left Aquila and Priscilla there, and then set off first for Jerusalem and then for home, in Antioch.

This would be his longest sea voyage—Ephesus to Caesarea. Perhaps he had another shipwreck of the three mentioned in his third letter to the Corinthians (our 2 Corinthians). Luke is meticulous about mentioning by name the many ports that the apostles came to on their sea journeys, but there is no mention of the three shipwrecks that 2 Corinthians speaks of. Luke gives us no indication that Paul suffered a shipwreck on this voyage, but somehow, before 56 A.D., he had experienced three.

The text implies that Paul visited the Jerusalem church briefly before he made his way back to his home base in Antioch. He did not stay long, though.[17] If he did not have a shipwreck on his late voyage, then he actually spent close to two years without suffering any physical violence. And although travel is exhausting, he was probably feeling fresh and renewed. He also had a new purpose. After visiting Jerusalem, he took up the task of raising a gift for the poor in the church there.

Multiplication: Evidence of a Lesson Learned and Things to Come

Before we begin to look at Paul's third journey, it is interesting to note that at this point Luke takes off on a tangent in his narrative. In Acts 18:24–28, Luke tells us about some events that took place in Ephesus and beyond. From Acts 13 on, the narrative focuses only on Paul. There is no further mention of Peter or Barnabas, and from this point on Luke doesn't even include Silas in the story. But for some reason, Luke launches into the story of a new character—Apollos.

Apollos was an Alexandrian Jew who was a great orator and a master of the Old Testament Scriptures. Apollos was acquainted with John the Baptist and knew of Jesus. Priscilla and Aquila had heard him in the synagogue and were greatly impressed but noticed that he didn't have the whole story yet. Therefore, they invited him to a private occasion and explained the fullness of the Gospel, including the death, burial, and resurrection of Jesus and the baptism of faith.[18] Apollos gladly received this fuller explanation and immediately wanted to go out to share the news with others. The church wrote him a letter commending him to the brothers and sisters in Achaia, and off he went. Luke says he helped the church in many ways and was powerful in refuting "the Jews in public, demonstrating by the Scriptures that Jesus was the Christ."

Why would Luke, with his already full parchment, set aside Paul's mission and take space for this tangent?[19] It is my belief that this is not a tangent but rather a magnifying glass, looking more closely at the results of Paul's lesson taught to him by Jesus in Corinth. Luke is showing us the effects of multiplying leadership from the harvest to the third generation. Paul found Aquila and Priscilla in the harvest and taught them the way while reasoning in the synagogue about the evidence of Jesus as Messiah. Then this couple went on to find Apollos and did the same with him. The paragraph ends with Apollos in turn doing the same, using language very similar to the language that describes Paul's ministry to the Jews (Acts 17:2–3). At this point, Apollos had not yet met Paul, but he was reproducing his methodology effectively because Paul had multiplied himself.[20]

Compare the language Luke uses to describe Paul's evangelistic method with the language he uses for that of Apollos:

Luke's Account of Paul's Evangelistic Method	Luke's Account of Apollos's Evangelistic Method
" . . . and according to Paul's custom	
he [Paul]	" . . . he [Apollos]
went to them [the Jews]	powerfully refuted the Jews
and for three Sabbaths	in public
reasoned with them from the Scriptures	demonstrating by the Scriptures
saying, 'This Jesus whom I am proclaiming to you is the Christ'" (Acts 17:2–3).	that Jesus was the Christ" (Acts 18:28).

Lessons of the Second Journey

The apostle Paul is a special man in history, but that is because he was open to the work God wanted to do in his life—both through him and in him. Paul is consistently put forth for us as an example of someone we can and should follow (Philippians 3:17; 2 Timothy 1:13, 2:2; 1 Corinthians 4:16–17, 11:1), and so it is important that we recognize commonalities between his life development and our own—and there are many. His journeys into Christlikeness are much like the path that we all must follow. On his second journey, Paul went through many of the learning cycles that all leaders must pass through if they hope to finish well.

Breaking with a Mentor—and Coming Back

At a critical point in Paul's development, he had a falling out with Barnabas, his mentor and friend. Dr. Charles Ridley, considered by many to be the father of modern-day assessment of church planters, founded his method on a simple idea: the best predictor of future behavior is past behavior. It appears that Paul held closely to the same philosophy regarding John Mark. Barnabas, by contrast, was quite familiar with the potential and power of a changed life, as amply demonstrated by his confidence in Paul's conversion and transformation.

Having been given such a long leash of leadership on his first journey, Paul was now confident that he knew what was necessary in order to conduct the mission correctly the second time around, and he was not going to let the same mistakes be repeated. This meant that John Mark was not getting a second chance.

On their second journeys, emerging leaders often show less respect for their mentor leaders as they step out on their own to do things their own way. This phase usually lasts about a year. We call it the *adolescent rebellion syndrome* (ARS). If mentors respond graciously, they will have even more respect afterward.

Several times over the last two decades, I have experienced this phenomenon in a way that was up close and personal. I have had apprentices speak poorly about me behind my back, in the hope of taking over leadership and/or churches (which I would gladly have given them anyway). I have heard vicious and untrue accusations tossed around by people I would have considered some of my closest friends. I've even seen one person poison the relationships I had with pre-Christians so that he could get full credit for the work. It often remains the case, however, that this syndrome is about methodology and philosophy of ministry. For example, I had one leader reject outright all my training regarding disciple making, leadership development, and organic church life (the same leader was also a poster child for my training's effectiveness) in favor of preaching sermons and starting up Sunday school classes.

All these episodes were hard, but the loss of relationships that had once been close was the most painful. In each case, I had been mentoring the apprentice with great intensity for a long time until suddenly, without notice or reason, all phone calls and connections came to an abrupt and cold end.

I did not coin the term *adolescent rebellion syndrome* and apply it in this manner, but my friend and mentor Ralph Moore did. Ralph founded the Hope Chapel movement, which now numbers hundreds of churches all over the world. He has raised and sent out more church planters than anyone else I can talk to in a Western context. Therefore, it was God's grace that at a crucial moment, when I was experiencing a nightmare of rejection by another beloved friend, that I had a chance to chat with Ralph about it. He smiled and told me that ARS occurs when an emerging leader is suddenly given the role of primary leader and steps out of the shadow of the mentor. Suddenly, it seems, the IQ of the mentor drops 100 points.

I am so grateful for that brief moment with Ralph. Fifteen minutes during a car ride, more than a decade ago, have borne much fruit in my life, and I hope to share it with you. Ralph described exactly what I had been experiencing over and over. He then gave me outstanding advice. His words, as best my memory can reconstruct them, were something like this: "When the emerging leader suddenly has no respect for you, do not get offended and retaliate with defensiveness or a lack of respect in return. Be the grown-up. Just as a parent will love their own child through any rebellion, show love, support, and compassion even in the face of what feels like hatred. This is very much like Jesus, who faced the vilest rebellion from the loved ones he trained. He was betrayed, abandoned, and denied by his apprentices, yet his love for them never diminished." After Ralph let this truth seep in, he added even more wisdom born of experience. He told me that when a mentor loves an apprentice through the phase of ARS, within a year the apprentice will come back, usually in tears, and the relationship will be restored and can even become deeper. If the mentor reacts to ARS by turning on the apprentice, the relationship may never be restored. Then he emphasized, "Remain the parent in the relationship. Don't be childish."

I am ashamed to admit that even after hearing this wise counsel, a couple years later I turned my back on Ralph for a season. After a year of not communicating with him, I wrote him a very sincere apology for my silence and for pulling away. He proved to be the gracious mentor that he challenged me to be. He is the real deal.

Several years and many apprentice leaders later, I still find his counsel on ARS to ring true. For some reason ARS always lasts a year, and after a year of loving someone who does not return the love, something happens. The person comes back. I have had leaders weep in my office and confess the things they have done to me that I didn't even know about at the time. I had another leader say, "I don't know *what* I was thinking!" Why ARS lasts for just a year, I don't know; that's for someone else to investigate. But I can confirm that this is true in most cases.

ARS simply describes a general tendency, not an absolute rule. Not everyone struggles with it, and not everyone returns after a year—or ever, for that matter. I am painting this picture with broad but realistic strokes but do not claim that ARS is universal.

While Paul and Barnabas were back in Antioch, there was a lot of tension. As I mentioned before, the first fissure in their relationship probably occurred when Barnabas pulled away from dining with the Gentiles in Antioch (Galatians 2:11–13). That could well have been the start of Paul's lack of respect, which developed into a full-blown case of ARS. Then they had a methodological disagreement over who should be on the team for the next journey. Not only did Paul and Barnabas separate, they also heard about the departure from grace of the new churches they had recently started. It is likely at this time that Paul wrote to them in what became his epistle to the Galatians. A look at the letter that Paul wrote is also revealing of his place in life development.

The Galatian letter is Scripture and without error in its original writing. I love the truth contained within it and have committed much of it to memory and leaned heavily on its potent strength through the years. Nevertheless, a most amazing thing about Scripture is the way God allows the human perspective and context to be part of the holy writ. You can read the New Testament letters and see differences in style and personality. You can pick up on the diverse contexts in which they were written. None of these unique human contributions takes anything away from Scripture; in fact, they are used by the Holy Spirit to make the word of God more powerful and real to us, we who also face real human situations.

That said, I notice that the voice of Paul in this early letter is far more forceful and dogmatic than in later ones. You can see that the letter, written by a younger Paul facing a situation with a degree of stubborn youthfulness, has a less forgiving tone. This takes nothing away from the truth of Galatians. God used it because that is exactly the tone the letter needed to have. This is merely an observation that some aspects of the styles of Paul's letters can be attributed to the maturation level of the human author. And why not? If a personal style of writing can be factored into Scripture without threatening its inspiration and inerrancy, then why can't we discern something of the human author's own place in the maturation process? It is common for someone who has completed the first journey and is preparing for the second to have a more self-assured, black-and-white view of the world. After the pain and formation of the second and then the third journey of life have chipped off some of the hard edges, a more subtle and yet equally truthful voice may come through. Galatians is not a lesser book for having been written by a less mature Paul. God sovereignly brought about this important issue at a time in Paul's life when he was perfectly equipped to write the letter that we would all need.

Paul had to mature, just as the rest of us do. It is not wrong to be immature, but it is wrong to remain immature. One cannot be faulted for being at the level of maturity that is natural in one's progression. The problem lies in *not* progressing. We may applaud the off-balance first steps of a young child when the child is less than a year old. When a thirty-year-old woman staggers the same way, we suspect that something is not right. What may be exceptional for a baby is cause for concern with an adult. No one faults a ten-year-old for being dependent on his parents, but when he is fifty and still living at home, unemployed or unemployable, there is a problem. Paul would be more mature on his later journeys, but that does not mean he was wrong to have the characteristics of a first- or second-journey leader during that time. The same is true for you. It is not bad to go through the second journey; it is unfortunate to remain in it and not move on to the third journey.

Learning to Surrender to God's Plan

On the second journey, Paul and Silas headed off by land to revisit the churches started on the first journey (Acts 15:41). They more than likely wanted to discover if those churches had responded well to Paul's letter. During this part of the journey, Timothy joined the team. I imagine that this was a joyful time of getting reacquainted, and we can hope that the churches of Galatia responded well to Paul's letter and to his second visit. I also imagine that Paul was anxious to launch out beyond the territory they had already reached. When they finally transitioned from the churches that were already established and walked into the spiritually uncharted fields of Asia Minor, they ran straight into the anguish of being told not to speak the word to Asians. Try to imagine the frustration Paul and his band would have felt traveling through a region full of lost people and not being allowed to preach the message that they all would gladly have died for. And they didn't know why the Lord was commanding them not to preach.

Then they were not even allowed to enter into Bithynia. And all they could do was walk on and on until they reached the sea. I imagine that they felt a lot like Moses when they reached the sea, unable either to go north or south or to retreat. Second-journey leaders often find that their plans, no matter how good, are not God's plans. The more quickly they learn to listen and follow, the better off they will be. It is at this stage of development that a leader must surrender to the Lord of the harvest and let go of all the plans that seemed so perfect.

God never downloads the whole plan at once; you have to discover it along the way. This is because the greater goal is not that we accomplish something but that we grow more intimate with our Lord. Those who listen well to God will find that God listens well to them, and they will accomplish a lot more.

In the 1990s, as director of church planting for my denomination in our region, I received many church-planting proposals from eager second-journey leaders, and yet I have never seen any of those proposals actually fulfilled as planned. God doesn't want us to feel as if we can do this on our own, nor does He want us to feel that it is our place to plan how His church is built.

About a year after my first church plant (while I was still functioning as director of church planting), I received a proposal from an emerging leader I had been mentoring. His name was Brad Fieldhouse. He had just finished his Master of Divinity degree from Fuller and had taken a class with Bob Logan in which he was to develop his church-planting proposal. He received a good grade on it and turned it in to his denominational leaders, who were very excited about it and wanted to support him. Then he came to me and presented it to me in my office. It was almost an inch thick, full of demographic studies of his targeted area's people, and it included a plan for strategic resource allocation and a flowchart showing how people would go from being lost to being deployed as leaders in the church. (Well, actually, I am just assuming that this is what was in the proposal, since I never actually read it.)

Brad handed me the proposal and asked if I would give him some feedback. He once described that meeting in this way: "I handed Neil the proposal, and he said, 'Thanks' and immediately turned and dropped it in the trash can beside his desk." That is what I did, and Brad, shocked and confused, said, "If you don't have time for it, I will understand."

I said to him, "I have time. I just don't want to read it right now. More importantly, I want *you* to be free of it. You see, we know that church-planting proposals never describe what happens. What we really want to see is that church planters know how to think strategically, and I already know that about you, Brad. This will serve you better than any proposal devised in isolation, away from the actual mission field. I have never seen one of these proposals come to fruition. What is in this proposal and what is out there on the streets will be very different, and the sooner you realize it, the freer you will be. That is why I just threw your hard work in the trash. I did it for you."[21]

Later Brad said that this was the most helpful advice he received before he began to start churches. The network of organic churches he started, called CrossRoads, did not look like the church he described in his proposal. It was much better because he went into the field listening to what God wanted him to do rather than trying to fulfill a plan. It is not bad to have a plan; it is bad to be cemented to your plan, without any flexibility. As I said to Brad, I am more interested in seeing how strategically you can think than I am in the actual plan you can come up with. A strategic thinker who listens closely to the Lord of the harvest is a powerful agent in God's kingdom.

William Faulkner once said, "In writing, you must kill all your darlings." This is actually good advice to anyone who wants to grow and mature in a craft. When I was an undergraduate art major, my drawing teacher used to say, "Your first good drawing will not be done until after your first twenty-five thousand drawings have been finished. Any great drawings will come much later than that." Second-journey leaders must learn to overcome their successes, and this can actually be a greater challenge than overcoming failures. We must be willing to kill our darling plans and methods if we hope to find even better ones. Sometimes a good plan is the enemy of the best one.

The Necessity of Suffering

In the coastal town of Troas, Paul added Luke to his team and finally received the marching orders from His lord that he desired. They set sail for Philippi and had the wind at their back, but it would not be all smooth sailing. In Philippi, they discovered that God's plan involved great pain in its fulfillment.

Why? Why is it that God would have us endure pain in order to fulfill his plan for our lives? The New Testament provides lots of good answers to this question:

- God loves us, and so He disciplines us. Sin is really that bad, and we need to understand, not just cognitively but also experientially, that it has consequences (Hebrews 12:4–11).

- The world, the flesh, and the devil hate Jesus, and so they hate us (John 15:18–25; 2 Timothy 3:10–12; 1 Peter 5:8–10) and do all they can to destroy us.

- God wants to get our attention, and so sometimes He has to break us to the point where we are able to listen and learn. Some things are truly learned only when accompanied by hurt. The pain solidifies the lesson in deep places in our lives (Hebrews 5:7–9; 1 Peter 5:8–10).

- God prepares us for greater fruitfulness by making space for more of Him in our lives. Suffering can teach us character and rid us of lesser things. Only when we rid ourselves of lesser props and supports do we lean more on God and develop a desperate dependence on Him (John 15:1–11; 1 Peter 4:1–3; James 1:2–4).

- The Gospel is truly worth dying for, and suffering demonstrates that—to ourselves and to those around us. Suffering can draw out and display the goodness in us and prove—to God, ourselves, and the world—that we are truly His followers. In this way, one can be a witness of His love in a context that magnifies His love in a compelling way (Matthew 5:10–12; 2 Timothy 1:7–11; 2 Timothy 2:2–10; 1 Peter 2:18–20, 3:14–17).

- God permits us to suffer so that we can have fellowship with Christ and know Him even in His suffering (Philippians 1:29, 3:10–11; John 15:18; Romans 8:17; Colossians 1:24; 1 Peter 2:21, 4:12–19). There are parts of Jesus that we cannot know without suffering.

- Our suffering prepares us to come to the aid and understanding of those who also suffer (Hebrews 2:17–18; 2 Corinthians 1:3–11). In suffering, we are being schooled to care for others who also suffer.

- We learn the love and comfort of our salvation when we realize the pain and suffering of this life. We begin to understand the price Jesus paid and value of the gift all the more because of the pain we have experienced in this cursed world, and we have more hope for the life that is to come (Romans 8:16–39).

All these answers are true, but they all fall short of satisfying the real heart (and hurt) behind the question. Perhaps the worst thing you could ever do is simply read this list of answers to someone who has suffered great loss. Writing them down on a sympathy card is not advised.

Greater minds than the one moving the fingers that type these words have addressed this subject more fully than this work will allow.[22] It may be better to suggest that pain is not an anomaly for the Christian, or a detour away from what God has in store for the faithful, but is actually the pathway for all godliness. We simply cannot become like the suffering Servant without suffering. If Jesus Himself had to learn obedience with suffering (Hebrews 5:7–9), how much more do we?

We should never just assume that we are suffering because God has left us or is angry with us. That is rarely the case, and it is certainly not the case for the children of God. He may discipline us, but it is because of His love, and it is for our own good. But suffering happens for many more reasons than discipline. It was President Theodore Roosevelt who said, "Never throughout history has a man who lived a life of ease left a name worth remembering." Hardship is what makes the story of our lives more compelling in the telling.

The lesson for emerging leaders is not to be surprised when you encounter pain. If the Scriptures are to be believed, you should be concerned if you do *not* face difficult challenges and pain. Whom the Lord loves, He disciplines (Hebrews 12:7–11). It is those who are bearing fruit that He prunes, not as punishment but as an investment for them to bear greater fruit in the future (John 15:1–2). He tests the faith of His followers to develop perseverance and joy (James 1:2–4). Learning is a pain, but it's worth it in the end.

Learning from What Works and What Doesn't

When Paul and his team hit the shores of Macedonia, they immediately set out to start churches and to implement the plan Paul had come up with to compensate for the problems from the first journey that had resulted in weak churches. He recruited more leaders and planned to leave one behind with each new church plant. The Lord let Paul follow through with this plan so that he could discover a better way. Jesus also used Paul's endeavors throughout Macedonia to establish His reign there. Paul did not fail in what he was doing—the Philippian and Thessalonian churches were some of the healthiest, to judge only from the contents of their epistles—but there was a better way that Paul had yet to learn.

It is dangerous these days to suggest that the great apostle Paul actually made mistakes. Perhaps I am overstating it; perhaps they were not really mistakes but forward progress in a valuable education. I believe that many, wanting to almost worship the apostle, have actually stripped him of one of his most admirable qualities—his openness to learning. The Scriptural text does not deify Paul, as we tend to do, but actually shows us all of his growth. We tend to read his life as a whole, and we sum up his patterns and decisions as if he had nothing to learn but already knew how to do everything. Paul himself does not make such claims; quite the opposite. He states clearly that he is trying to learn and grow in his maturation (Philippians 3:12–16). Perhaps if we can recapture Paul's journeys of development, we can see him in a new light and learn even more from him. This is the hope behind the book you are reading now. It is virtually impossible to find a mature leader of great significance who cannot point to lessons learned through trial and error. Let us grant Paul the same courtesy.

Listening in a Season of Aloneness and Fear

After Paul landed in Athens and his guides left him, he realized the short-comings of his strategy. Even in a city full of people, noise, and activity, one can feel alone. For many emerging leaders, there is a need to be isolated for a time. In this case, it wasn't the sort of extended isolation that Paul had endured in Tarsus. It was a brief time of loneliness, just enough to get his attention and communicate a new profound truth. In a real sense, there are many moments when God is speaking, but the noise in our busy lives is too loud for us to really hear and understand. It is at those times that God may actually intentionally turn down the volume of other voices, especially our own, just so we can have ears to hear what He has to say. This may seem to happen only when we have difficult challenges that cause us to stop, look, and listen.

Jesus had actually instructed the disciples in this idea of staying in a place longer when He taught the seventy before sending them out. He said, "And if a man of peace is there your peace will rest upon him. . . . *Stay in that house [oikos], eating and drinking what they give you. . . . Do not keep moving from house to house*" (Luke 10:6–7; emphasis added). Jesus wants the Gospel to spread from house to house, doesn't He? Why, then, does He command the disciples to stay rather than move on? It is because He wants the Gospel to move from house to house, not the missionary. When the missionary does all the work, it creates a dependency on the missionary and the new disciples are less empowered and less likely to carry on the work. An indigenous viral movement can only happen if it spreads from "carrier" to "carrier," naturally, without dependence on the missionary. While instructing the twelve in missional practices, He also said, "And into whatever city or village you enter, inquire who is worthy in it [find a person of peace]; and *abide there until you go away*" (Matt. 10:11; emphasis added). Apparently this idea of staying longer was not understood by the disciples . . . at least until now.

Jesus knew what Paul had to learn from the beginning but needed the right time to instruct him so that the lesson would change everything. Sometimes it takes pain and personal crisis to awaken us to learn things in a deep and meaningful way. There are levels of learning. Being able to hear information and simply pass a test is a shallow level. Applying the idea personally is a little deeper. But when something is learned through frustration and failure, the lesson is learned in a life-changing way. When we then apply our learning and teach it to others, we own it on a deep and personal level, and it becomes cemented in our lives permanently. There is no doubt that we are all better learners when we face the painful shortcomings of our own strategies. Jesus will let us go on with our own plans, and will likely even bless the efforts, all the while waiting to reveal a better way when our hearts are prepared to hear in the deepest part. He is still saying, "He who has ears to hear, let him hear."

The second journey, typically, is not just about refining strategy, although refinement is needed. It isn't just about developing character, but of course character is developed. It is a both/and struggle. When we make the Christian experience only about character, we make the mistake of thinking that what we do doesn't matter—but it does. When we make the Christian life only about methodology, it loses all liveliness and power and becomes an empty shell. Of course, character is the foundation on which methodology has its impact. One can preach beyond one's character, but one cannot develop as a disciple beyond one's character. We can truly go only as far in our spiritual journey as our character will allow. Godliness is the life that fills the methodology with breath and a beating heart. I believe, however, that we must be open to the fact that God does not simply want to change our hearts but may also, in the process, want to teach us how to better do His work.

One thing I think leaders must be delivered from while on their journeys to significance is their own success. When we see fruitfulness in earlier journeys, we tend to institutionalize the methods that brought about that success, and we end up stuck. We cannot move forward until we are dissatisfied with our current state.

If a lesson is never learned, the leader can get caught in the cycle of learning the same painful lesson over and over again. The pain gets increasingly unbearable, until finally the leader quits and opts for an easier, more placid life and becomes less able to hear God's voice. Such leaders live out their lives absorbed in the machinations of ministry, devoid of the spark of life that comes when God's voice and leading are heard. Don't let that happen to you. It is one of the ways a leader can hit a plateau and fall short of finishing well.

Here are some practical ideas for the second-journey leader:

1. Don't try to be someone else. It is common for younger leaders to admire and emulate more seasoned veterans of ministry. This is a good thing, but along the way we must become the man or woman God intends for us to be and not strive to be someone else.

2. Hold very lightly to your plans and strategies. In fact, I often suggest that new church planters take their proposed plans and actually have a worship service where they offer them up literally in a bonfire and ask God to lead them into the work out in the field. How sad it is when I encounter missionaries who have been hard at work for years, often decades, and who are not open to veering at all from whatever plans they developed before they got on the ground. Some people, to their detriment and the detriment of all who would follow them, cling to their plans more tightly than they cling to the imminent and intimate presence of Jesus.

3. Don't think that because you are a beloved Christian, suffering isn't part of the plan. Suffering may not be welcomed, but it should also not be a surprise.

4. Don't take a cheap route. Shortcuts in character formation result in shortcomings in character. Trying to avoid pain can actually take you off the path God has for you. It is better to move forward into what God has for you than to relieve your pain for a moment. It is the desire to escape pain in life that leads a good many people into all sorts of evil. Escape is not the solution; endurance is. The fear of further pain can keep the leader from further learning. It is far better to discover God's grace in the midst of suffering than to avoid suffering entirely.

5. Don't let the lessons learned from the pain become the sole platform of your life and a distraction that prevents the next journey. Rejoice in the lessons learned, but keep on learning. Never be content to remain in your current state. Press forward.

The lessons of the second journey are learned through conflict, frustration, pain, mistakes, loneliness, and fear. You can't skip the second journey and hope to finish well. When you pass through the lessons of the second journey, a whole new journey awaits, one of greater expansive influence than you can imagine.

CONVERGENCE
AND
AFTERGLOW

PART THREE

The temple for Caesar worship from Pergamum where a church was started in Paul's third journey. It was here that Jesus said the throne of Satan was found.

The theater in Ephesus today. This is where the angry mob assembled. In the foreground is the Arcadian Way, leading to the docks of the port of Ephesus.

5

The Third Journey
Convergence in Ephesus

*Try not to become a man of success but
rather to become a man of value.*
—Albert Einstein

*A wide door for effective service has opened to me,
and there are many adversaries.*
—the apostle Paul describing his third journey (1 Corinthians 16:9)

THERE IS A MOMENT IN THE lives of some leaders when all their training, experience, learning, character formation, calling, and giftedness merge into a potent and very fruitful combination. J. Robert Clinton refers to this phase of maturity as "convergence." During convergence, he says, "God moves a leader into a role that matches his or her gift-mix and experience so that ministry is maximized."[1]

Not every leader has the privilege of experiencing this phase of life. Because of the apparent high cost of character formation, many give up on the growth process in earlier phases of development and simply live out their lives in less fruitful stages of maturity. But those who pay the price and continue until they reach this point become highly effective, with expanding influence. Our greatest significance awaits us at the end of much pain and many hard lessons. No one who truly influences the world in a lasting way over the course of a lifetime does so easily.

Once a leader steps into the convergence of the third journey, he or she will recognize that all the previous journeys were preparation for what comes later. To reach a peak in your success earlier in life is in some ways a tragedy of opportunity missed. All of us long for success throughout our lives, but we should long to see greater significance later in life and not see it wasted on our younger years. Success, in and of itself, is a heavy burden to bear; to bear it without a firm foundation of maturity and strong character can lead to great personal destruction.

I often look at young starlets who reach the peak of their lives in their early twenties and feel much sadness and grief as I see them stumble ahead into dark depression with the realization that their best days are behind them, before they have even reached the age of twenty-five. Even as I write this, one movie star still in her twenties is being equipped with a court-ordered ankle bracelet that monitors her whereabouts. Mug shots of young celebrities in orange jumpsuits, like photos of forgotten child actors dying young, have become clichés. It is quite common to find that people in such a state turn to self-medication to numb the painful reality that they will spend the rest of their lives looking back at an early peak. For the rest of their lives they will be known as the ones who "used to be somebody." That is a heavy burden for anyone to live with, but especially for someone who didn't have a chance to develop the depth of character necessary to bear such a load.

Success built simply on talent, in the absence of the necessary substance of true, hard-won character, will always be short-lived and does not lead to personal fulfillment. Life will pimp your talent and suck it out of you, if you let it, leaving you with deep loneliness and regrets.

Perhaps the only thing sadder than a young starlet with her best days behind her is an old man still dressing up in skin-tight leather pants and strutting about a stage, singing the songs that made him famous thirty years ago. A man like that has not developed as an artist and is stuck singing the same old songs, over and over again, to thinning crowds with thinning hair and thickening waists.

It is actually quite rare, but possible, to find artists who develop and continue to mature as the years go by. These artists have several "greatest hits" on multiple CDs that are labeled by decades, each with a more mature and progressive creativity that comes from a life well lived. The people who buy their music are usually a much wider and growing group because these artists not only keep the old audience but win a new one with ever-newer expressions of their art. These artists not only change their own art, they advance the art form itself. The reason their art is advancing is that they themselves are developing and progressing. Their art reflects their own growth and maturity, and so it resonates with us in a far deeper way because it captures the essence of life itself.

As I mentor young people, I always try to encourage them to find their best years ahead so that they are not content with early success but continue to push through pain and hardship to find their greatest significance later in life. The truth is, if you live for success, you will not reach a level of maturity where true convergence occurs. You must live for something more important than mere success, something that will compel you from within to press on. You need a hunger within that is not content with lesser things so you can keep moving forward through the challenges and come out with greater significance at the end.

Moses, Daniel, Joseph, John the Baptist, Paul, and even Jesus all had the silent years of which we know little except that those years were long, a period when these figures were mostly unknown. But the fact that those years were silent doesn't mean that they weren't full of important learning. In fact, what we learn in the quiet years is often the foundation for our more influential years.

Paul was willing to pay the price for greater impact in the future, and that was a wise choice. In the coastal city of Ephesus, he stepped into the convergence of all his life's journeys to find his spiritual authority, skill, and character all magnified in an extraordinary way. His resulting powerful influence did not come simply from of a new strategy or a new method. One cannot just pray into such effectiveness. This sort of fruitfulness is paid for in the course of the journeys of life. It is the return on one's investment of hard work and painful struggle.

Paul's Third Journey

Having learned the hard lessons of the second journey, and no longer forbidden by the Holy Spirit to preach the message, Paul was now ready to go to Asia. The text does not say that Paul had a partner with him on this journey. We are left to guess where Silas was deployed. Barnabas was off on his own adventure. Paul, with only the apprentices he had picked up on his second missionary journey (Acts 19:22, 29), passed through the Galatian region, strengthening the disciples there yet again (Acts 18:23), and then headed straight to Ephesus, the most influential city of Asia Minor.

On his first journey, Paul covered 1,500 miles in one year. On this third journey, he lived almost exclusively in Ephesus for three years (Acts 20:31), but the word of God spread in an incredible way to cover more than 4,000 square miles. In fact, the success of this missionary journey is hard to fathom. Luke says that everyone who was in Asia, Jew and Gentile alike, heard the word of the Lord. That is an incredibly fruitful mission trip in only three years, especially in view of the fact that Paul never even ventured out of the city of Ephesus. How did he do it?

The Holy Spirit in Acts

After revisiting (for at least the fourth time) the churches from his first journey, Paul landed in Ephesus and encountered a group of "disciples." He immediately noticed, however, that something significant was lacking. He inquired whether they had received the Holy Spirit when they came to believe, and they informed him that they had never even heard of the Holy Spirit. With that information, Paul didn't preach about receiving the second blessing of the Holy Spirit but instead preached the Gospel of Jesus. And when they believed, he laid hands on them and they were filled with the Holy Spirit.

I often wonder whether Paul, if he were to visit our churches today, wouldn't see something missing right away. We often make church about what we can do, with or without the Holy Spirit. Our personalities, musical abilities, programs, and buildings are usually far more noticeable than the fruit of the Spirit (Galatians 5:22–23).

Our Bibles call Luke's account the Acts of the Apostles, but really it should be called the Acts of the Holy Spirit. I've counted fifty-seven occasions in the twenty-eight chapters of Acts on which the Holy Spirit is addressed in some manner. In the book of Acts, the Holy Spirit is immediately noticeable. His presence is noticed on the first day (Acts 2:5–13). Even the enemies of the disciples notice the Spirit of Jesus in them (Acts 4:13). Leaders at that time were chosen on the basis of how recognizable the Holy Spirit was in their lives (Acts 6:3). The Gentile's salvation was verified by the immediate presence of the Holy Spirit (Acts 11:15–18).

Equally significant were those times when the Holy Spirit was not evident, such as among the Samaritans before the commissioning of Peter and John (Acts 8:14–24). And now, in Ephesus, Paul immediately recognized that something was wrong (Acts 19:1–7).

I am not sure that we are able to recognize the presence (or absence) of the Holy Spirit as readily as they did in the New Testament. It was not the gifts (whether tongues or something else) that really made a spirit-filled church recognizable. The Corinthian church had every gift (1 Corinthians 1:7) but was carnal and full of divisions (1 Corinthians 3:2–4) and even immorality (1 Corinthians 5:1–2). Gifts are not as important as the fruit of the Spirit. One can use one's gifts in a selfish manner, but one cannot exhibit love in a selfish way.

Whenever a list of spiritual gifts is talked about in the New Testament, love is mentioned in a very conspicuous manner. Is love the most noticeable thing, which people pick up on immediately when they come to your church? We need more of the Spirit and less of ourselves in the way we function as churches. Spiritual gifts are wonderful, but the greatest gift is love (1 Corinthians 12:31–13:3).

Paul's Work in Ephesus

As was his pattern, after Paul arrived in Ephesus, he began to preach in the synagogue and did so for three months until the Jews finally had enough and forced him out. He then found another place to meet, where he could preach the Gospel in public—the school of Tyrannus. We do not know much about the man Tyrannus, but his name is mentioned in the archaeological finds of Ephesus, and so his actual existence is verified in extrabiblical sources. Perhaps he was a philosophical teacher who had a school that rented space to Paul. The Western text (an ancient manuscript on which the King James translation is based) includes an additional line that says that Paul would meet there and teach from eleven in the morning until four in the afternoon. This is actually quite plausible, given that those midday hours are when most of the people in the city would have rested, to escape the hot sun. It has been said that more Ephesians would have been awake at one in the morning than at one in the afternoon.[2] Paul may have worked in the morning hours as well as later in the afternoon, making tents (Acts 20:35). Then, while most of the city was resting, he would have done the exhausting work of training the new disciples and the emerging leaders. He followed this pattern for two full years, probably from the fall of 52 A.D. to the summer of 55 A.D.[3]

Ephesus, situated where the Cayster River meets the Aegean Sea, was a center for commercial enterprise, and although it competed with Pergamum for political influence, there is no doubt that, culturally and commercially, it was the leading city of the region.[4] One of the seven wonders of the ancient world was in this highly influential city—the temple of Artemis. This gigantic temple, with 127 columns, stood 60 feet tall and was 425 feet long and 220 feet wide and dwarfed all else in the city, both physically and culturally.[5] Today there is nothing left of this grand edifice save for a single reconstructed column that remains alone in a muddy field.

Ephesus was world famous for this temple, and for the worship of Artemis, a Greek goddess of the hunt, wild animals, wilderness, childbirth, virginity, and young girls, who was believed to bring and relieve disease in women. The people believed that the statue of Artemis in the temple had simply fallen from the sky, and that Ephesus was its guardian.

With this sort of belief in Artemis, the city was captivated by superstition. The temple was not just a commercial enterprise (although it was certainly that) but also created a spiritual identity that held the hearts and minds of the people in bondage to fear and superstition.

Magic, including spells and charms, was a big part of the culture of Ephesus. Ironically, a renowned magical item, which carried a written charm, was called the Ephesian Letters. They were not really much more than a series of words for chanting and casting spells, and they were treated like good-luck charms.[6] God in His wisdom, and with a sly sense of humor, has given us Paul's Ephesian letter, which carries true power that is ours in Christ and is a true sword of the spirit against the demonic forces we face. In this dark environment, Paul set out to instigate a spiritual uprising throughout Asia that would overthrow evil and establish a work that could not be stopped.

Paul knew that we cannot simply enter a place and see it as only a material world. There is a spiritual world that is just as real, and that influences our lives profoundly, although we are often blind to it. Ignoring it will not produce significant results in either world. Our efforts on behalf of God's kingdom are to be effective in both the material and the spiritual realm. That was the case at Ephesus. The Gospel overturned the dark strongholds of this city and set people free from their bondage to the occult. Paul saw wondrous miracles occur through his life in Ephesus that revealed to all that there is indeed a more powerful way of living one's life.

Those who had position, and who had profited from the worship of Artemis, understood that Paul was a direct threat to their way of life. They commented, "Not only is there danger that this trade of ours fall into disrepute, but also that the temple of the great goddess Artemis be regarded as worthless and that she whom all of Asia and the world worship will even be dethroned from her magnificence" (Acts 19:27). In this spiritual warfare, there would be a winner and a loser. Those who had a vested interest in the old system understood that this was a spiritual fight for the soul of Asia. Often those in a place who have a vested interest in the strongholds of evil are more acutely aware than even those in the church of the threat that the kingdom of God brings. Today in this place there is hardly anything left of the cult of Artemis worship as it was in Paul's day, but the true Ephesian letter that Paul wrote is still as powerful in changing lives as when it was first written.

When Paul later wrote to the Ephesians, he reminded them that it had been a spiritual war: "For our struggle is not against flesh and blood, but against the rulers, against the powers, against the spiritual forces of wickedness in the heavenly places" (Ephesians 6:12). The Bible clearly teaches us that we have an adversary, a spiritual being that rules over the demonic world that we do not see. In his letter to the Ephesians, Paul calls this being "the prince of the power of the air" (Ephesians 2:2). It may feel as if Satan is everywhere at once and all-knowing, but only Almighty God is. Nevertheless, Satan does have an army of demonic forces at his command that is dispersed in all the cities and places where people live.

When Paul entered Asia Minor to expand the reign of Christ by setting spiritual captives free from this demonic rule, he entered into perhaps the most hostile spiritual environment in the world at that time. When Jesus, in the Book of Revelation, spoke to the churches that were begun during this journey, he acknowledged something spiritual in the region that bears observation here. Seventy-five miles north of Ephesus is the city of Pergamum. Jesus, in writing to this church, boldly stated that it was here, in Pergamum, that Satan dwelled (Revelation 2:13). He mentioned that the throne of Satan was there, and many speculate that it may be the grand altar built to Zeus that sat atop the highly fortified acropolis of Pergamum.[7]

This new work in Asia faced extremely harsh spiritual conflicts. Perhaps that fact offers a clue to why the Lord forbade Paul to preach the Gospel in Asia before having learned the lessons of his second journey. This delay was not only about strategy but also about spiritual fortification in Paul's life and character.

In this spiritually dark and superstitious climate, Jewish magicians were also considered especially powerful. Because the Jews would not pronounce the name of God (to avoid using it in vain, and to keep the third of the Ten Commandments, as explained in Exodus 20:7), the Gentile world thought this meant that God's name carried extremely potent magic. In Ephesus, the expanding church would encounter its third representative of Jewish magicians, the first having been Simon in Samaria (Acts 8:9–13) and the second, Elymas in Cyprus (Acts 13:6–12). In Acts 19:13–20, the church encountered the seven sons of Sceva, who was himself purported to have been a high priest, the only one in Judaism who was allowed, once a year, to invoke the name of Yahweh. Today there are fragments of magical papyri from Ephesus that attempted to reproduce the true pronunciation of Yahweh in magic incantations. On a magical papyri now in the Bibliothèque Nationale in Paris, there is even a close approximation on what the sons of Sceva recited. It reads, "I adjure you by Jesus, the God of the Hebrews."[8] In the culture to which Paul was ministering, there was a combination of fear, jealousy, and loathing of Jews.[9]

In this place full of superstition and longing for spiritual power Paul showed up, and through his hands many were healed, and demonic spirits were cast out as people were set free by the Gospel. Even articles of clothing taken from Paul healed and released people from demonic bond-age (Acts 19:11). To a crowd that was accustomed to the magic arts, this must have been seen as powerful and dynamic.

Some others, when they cast spells, tried to evoke what they saw as Paul's magic by using the same words Paul had used. The seven sons of Sceva, who tried that in exorcising an evil spirit, discovered that Paul's words were not a magic incantation but a true reflection of something much greater, based on real spiritual authority, which they did not have. The demon acknowledged Jesus and Paul but then proceeded to beat and humiliate the seven sons. Paul's own spiritual authority was growing by the day. As people were released from captivity, they were immediately trained and deployed in God's service. When they believed and aban-doned sorcery, they soon realized that this new faith was far more power-ful than any magic.

These conversions became known throughout Ephesus when the new Christians collected all the magic parchments that the Ephesians had owned and burned them in a massive bonfire, to declare boldly and pub-licly that they would no longer remain enslaved to magic spells, curses, and charms.[10] It was not enough to have the Ephesians simply add Jesus to their current cultural and religious mind-set. The Gospel of Christ demanded an all-or-nothing surrender to Jesus as King. We are to take up our own cross and follow him as a requisite first step in our spiritual walk; anything less results in an anemic church that claims Christianity but shows none of the real thing. Once you have surrendered your life (which is all that carrying one's cross can allude to), it is easy to surrender your false gods and the devices of your former spiritual practice, even if doing so represents a great amount of money. In this case, it was equiva-lent to fifty thousand pieces of silver.

The Ephesians who made their living by making and selling the para-phernalia of superstition soon saw that this turn of events was bad for business and bad for the worship of Artemis, and so they instigated a riot and great confusion in the city. Many rushed into the large theater, chanting as one, "Great is Artemis of the Ephesians!" Try to imagine a large outdoor stadium full of twenty-five thousand energized people all shouting in one voice, "Great is Artemis of the Ephesians!" (I even imag-ine seeing a beach ball or two being bounced around, with an occasional "wave" initiated, and someone selling peanuts, but I'm a little too cre-ative.) Eventually, level heads prevailed, and the assembly of angry people disbanded and returned to their homes.[11]

Shortly after this mob dispersed, Paul went off to Macedonia and Greece in order to revisit the churches from the previous journey and then move on to Jerusalem to bring funds for relief of the famine there. After that mission was accomplished, his intent was to go to the capital of the world—Rome.

An Incredible Fruitfulness

This third missionary journey is set apart from the others by its amazing effectiveness. It is one thing to see the incredible results that occurred in Ephesus, but that was just the beginning. Churches were started all across Asia Minor during these three years.

The seven churches of Asia Minor mentioned in the opening chapters of Revelation are some of the fruit of this missional expedition. Not just Ephesus but also Smyrna, Pergamum, Thyatira, Sardis, Philadelphia, and Laodicea were likely started during these three years. Colossae and Hieropolis also owe their beginnings to this missionary journey. These Asian churches are set apart from the ones started during Paul's previous journeys by the fact that he himself didn't start them. Although he wrote the apostolic letter to the Colossian church, he did not start the church. In fact, he mentions that the Colossians have never even seen his face (Colossians 2:1). If Paul didn't start this church that he wrote to, who did? A man named Epaphras is likely the one who started the Colossian church (Colossians 1:6–8) as well as the churches in Hieropolis and Laodicea. Epaphras was a disciple of Paul's who was originally from the region of these three cities (Colossians 4:11–13), which are all very close to one another. He came to know Christ in Ephesus, received some hands-on mentoring there, and then returned to his homeland armed with the Gospel and a new apostolic call. He was so good at learning from his mentor that eventually we find him in jail beside Paul (Philemon 22).

Paul is considered the apostolic leader and the father (or grandfather) of all these churches. He refers to himself as "Paul, the aged" to Philemon, who hosted a church in his home in Colossae (Philemon 8–9). Although it was Epaphras who began the work, he also mentions that Philemon owes his own life to Paul and talks about the work he began in Asia (Philemon 17–20), even though the two may not have met. Paul learned to spread his apostolic foundation without needing to be present. He learned to work through others rather than doing it all himself. He learned this in the depths of the second journey, but he perfected it on the third one.

Epaphras was just one of many whom Paul trained and sent throughout Asia. It was such a profound work that Luke recounts the success of this missionary journey by stating emphatically that every single person who lived in Asia heard the message of God, whether Jew or Gentile (Acts 19:10). That is incredible. Even Paul's enemies said of him during this time, "You see and hear that not only in Ephesus, but in almost all of Asia, this Paul has persuaded and turned away a considerable number of people, saying that gods made with hands are no gods at all" (Acts 19:26).

The Inevitable Cost

One cannot see the kinds of powerful breakthrough in such a dark place as Ephesus without a cost, one that we must pay to be used in this way. Luke mentions little of the trials Paul endured on this journey, but there are still glimpses of it found in the New Testament. While reporting on his fruitful work in Ephesus and all of Asia to the Corinthians, Paul mentions that he faced some strong opposition (1 Corinthians 16:9). We might assume that he is referring to the incident with the mob at the theater, but I believe there was much more that Paul endured that is not mentioned in Acts. To the Corinthians he mentions even having to fight off wild beasts in Ephesus (1 Corinthians 15:32), perhaps alluding to a Roman form of entertainment in which prisoners were forced to face wild animals in the stadium to fight for their freedom. The burdens Paul had to face while working in Ephesus were so heavy that at one point he lost all his strength and even despaired of life itself (2 Corinthians 1:8–11). Taking on the throne of Satan and all the spiritual forces in Asia took its toll on the apostle. If he hadn't been prepared for this through the important character development and strategic lessons learned on the second journey, he might not have made it through the third one. This, I believe, is the likeliest reason why Paul was forbidden to preach the Gospel in Asia during his second journey. He needed the depth of character and the lessons in reproductive ministry that he would learn on that journey before he could survive his third journey.

After Asia

After Ephesus, Paul went to Macedonia and Greece. There is some evidence that when he went to Macedonia he also took the Egnatian Way west and then ventured up into Illyricum (modern Albania). We can conclude this on the basis of the fact that he mentioned to the Romans, in his letter to them written at the end of the third journey, that he had preached the Gospel as far as Illyricum (Romans 15:19). He does not appear to have ventured that far northwest on any previous journey, and this is the only gap of this journey where such a trip seems plausible. It appears that Paul had learned his new strategy well but was still an apostle who "aspired to preach the Gospel, not where Christ was already named" (Romans 15:20).

Later on this third journey, he is seen traveling with a band larger than ever. In fact, the members seem to represent all his church-planting efforts, and for good reason. Luke mentions Sopater of Berea, Aristarchus and Secundus of Thessalonica, Gaius and Timothy of Derbe/Lystra, Tychicus and Trophimus of Asia, and Luke. There is a strong possibility, based on other epistles, that Titus was also with the group (2 Corinthians 8:6–23, 12:18). Luke seems to leave all mention of Titus out of Acts, which begs the question of why. I believe it may be because he deserted Paul and went to Dalmatia because he loved the world more than the mission (2 Timothy 4:10).[12]

The best explanation of why Paul had so many traveling with him is that he was collecting funds from all the Gentile churches to distribute in Jerusalem for famine relief (1 Corinthians 16:3). Therefore, there were two very good reasons for such a delegation—to have representation from all the churches when the gift was delivered, and to discourage robbers from stealing what they had.

Insights into the Successes of Paul's Third Journey

Luke and the Holy Spirit, anticipating that we will wonder how Paul could have been so fruitful in such a short time, tell us, without veering from the narrative style of Acts. Luke presents us with more didactic information about this missionary journey by having Paul recount how he has done his work for the elders of the Ephesian church on a spiritual retreat in Miletus.

Selection of a Strategic Base Camp

Paul established a regional base camp of leadership formation in Ephesus, a world-class city that would have had the most trade and influence passing through its streets (Acts 19:9). Pergamum may have been the capital of the region, but Ephesus was the heart of the region commercially. It is not a stretch to believe that Paul would choose Los Angeles over Sacramento, and New York City over Albany; with this strategy, ultimately he would get Sacramento and Albany too. To those he trained he said, "You yourselves know, from the first day I set foot in Asia, how I was with you the whole time" (Acts 20:18).

Spiritual and Relational Authority

The personal attacks and trials he had endured conferred authority on Paul's life. His scars were a calling card for his apostleship, and those who followed Jesus respected him because of them. He would often point to them as the true evidence that he was indeed an apostle (2 Corinthians 4:8–12, 11:21–29; Galatians 6:17). The way he faced his trials, without shrinking from the cost of doing the work, showed the Ephesian elders that he was a man willing to pay the price many times over for what he believed. (Acts 20:19–20).

Paul gave the Holy Spirit His rightful place in leading disciples into ministry (Acts 20:28). On his first journey, he and Barnabas appointed elders (Acts 14:23), but after two additional journeys, Paul had a more seasoned outlook. Realizing that the responsibility for raising elders rested with the One who will always be there for the leaders, he reminds them that it was not he but the Holy Spirit who appointed them to lead. In a sense, Paul had no intention of returning to visit these churches several times, as he had needed to do with the Galatian churches (Acts 20:25).[13]

Although the Ephesian church's beginning was marked by the absence of the Holy Spirit, that was quickly corrected. The Holy Spirit's presence would soon mean everything in the life of this church and all that she would birth. He told them that they might not see Paul's face again (Acts 20:25) but that the Holy Spirit would always be present (Acts 20:32).

Paul labored among the people at his own trade. Some have questioned whether Paul's vocational work of making tents was helpful or actually detrimental to his church-planting efforts. They point out that the places where he spent so little time, such as Philippi and Thessalonica, had what appear to have been healthier churches, and that the places where he stayed and worked his trade had churches that were not as healthy, especially the Corinthian church. I have a different perspective.

In the first place, we have already pointed out that while Paul left Philippi and Thessalonica after only a short stay, he also left behind in each of these places a leader (Luke and Timothy) to help train the emerging church. The Galatian churches were started quickly and then left without any mentoring support. One can certainly argue that these first-journey churches were the weakest of his church plants and required more personal visits than any others.

The Corinthian church's troubles required a minimum of three letters from Paul, written to address some very serious problems.[14] It is true that Paul worked his trade there, but when Timothy and Silas rejoined him, he stopped making tents and started giving all his time to ministry while, supposedly, previous church plants provided some support (2 Corinthians 11:8) and his co-workers earned enough income to free him up to serve (Acts 18:5; 2 Corinthians 11:9). It appears that almost the opposite occurred in Ephesus, where Paul says he worked with his own hands the entire time to support even those who were on his apostolic team (Acts 20:34). I believe that this was a significant shift for Paul. The problems found in the Corinthian church certainly reflected the severe trials and temptations associated with its unique locale. If anything, however, there is evidence that Paul made tents there only for a short time and then poured himself full-time into the church work. Perhaps through trial and error, he realized the shortcomings of that strategy as well, so that when he went to Ephesus he did the opposite.

The establishment of the Ephesian church was remarkable in that it saturated an entire population with churches using common people. These people more than likely came into contact with Paul through their trades and probably continued in their work as they took the Gospel with them to their hometown and beyond. By working the way he did, Paul established a life pattern that they could all follow, and he set the tone for an all-volunteer movement.

Too often, some on missions who are fully supported are inefficient. Paul, however, showed that plying his trade full-time while also training indigenous leaders could work incredibly well. Perhaps the very things we think will make us more efficient actually keep us from achieving the effectiveness we long to see. Paul serves as a model of someone whose work for God is helped and not hindered by the ebb and flow of real life. Paul was able to ask more of those he trained, and they rose to the challenge, following his own example. He also established a mission work that was not dependent on the missionary, because it was not done by a fully supported professional. In this way, he did not set the bar so high that none of the indigenous leaders could emulate him.

Paul points back to his own hard work as a type of authority that comes by example so that others will follow. He says, "You yourselves know that these hands ministered to my own needs and to the men who were with me. In everything I showed you that by working hard in this manner you must help the weak and remember the words of the Lord Jesus, that He Himself said, 'It is more blessed to give than to receive'" (Acts 20:34–35). His hard work is also evidence that he was not serving out of questionable motives (Acts 20:33)—a demonstration that, I fear, is needed in our own world today.

Years of following Christ through the journeys of life will produce insight that cannot be faked or bought. We see a small glimpse of Paul's perspective, gained from years of experience, when he confidently replies to the elders, "I know that after my departure savage wolves will come in among you, not sparing the flock; and from among your own selves men will arise, speaking perverse things, to draw away the disciples after them" (Acts 20:29–30). These are not simply prophetic words. There are scars and many tears behind them.

Strategic One-to-One Training

Paul constantly mentored individuals on a one-to-one basis (Acts 20:31). He seemed to hold back nothing from his apprentices. Paul integrated learning, both in public settings, such as the school of Tyrannus, and in the settings where life took place, following the natural paths of life from household (*oikos*) to household (Acts 20:19–20). The spiritual formation of Paul's disciples had evangelism as a foundation for training in ministry (Acts 20:21). His apprentices learned truth not just studying or memorizing truth but also by obeying it. Nothing cements the truth of the Gospel in your own life like giving it away to others.

Paul mentored his apprentices by instruction—through public discussion (as in daily dialogue in the school of Tyrannus), personal admonition (Acts 20:31), and example (Acts 20:33–35). There is not one way to train people. We must be holistic in our approach to training leaders.

Raising Up Leaders

Paul developed indigenous leaders in such a way that they could carry on the work without needing his presence. They were deployed in service immediately. They were imprinted upon Christ alone from the first day they believed.

As we have discussed, some may be inclined to believe that leaving a place quickly, rather than remaining there to teach and lead, actually makes a leader more independent, but that is not the case. I am not arguing for lifelong service in one place for a missionary. I do not believe that anyone who actually has an apostolic gifting could do that anyway. But I am finding that if a church is started and the missionary leaves before leaders can be mentored and established, the church feels abandoned and inadequate, which fuels a desire for more dependency, not less. Jesus stayed with his band of leaders three years, and that is also how long Paul stayed in Ephesus. Perhaps we should look longer at this length of time for a pioneering missionary enterprise. Is it possible that Paul, having stayed a year and a half in Corinth, left when his work was only half done? Perhaps this also helps to explain the struggles of the Corinthian church after Paul left. It is from Ephesus that Paul writes his letters to the Corinthians. Addressing their problems may have prompted him to stay twice as long in Ephesus.

You can argue that Paul had an exit strategy even before he had an entrance strategy for Asia. It certainly appears that his stay for three years was planned (Acts 20:31). He empowered his leaders with accountability to God for the work that he modeled for them, and so his presence wasn't needed in order for the work to continue when he left (Acts 20:32). Paul released the power of God's word in people's lives to carry the grassroots movement of multiplication (Acts 19:20). This was not simply theory for the emerging leaders to learn after he departed. It was proved to them throughout the three years as Paul trained and sent apostolic church planters out all over Asia. They knew that what Paul had prepared them for was possible. They wept at the good-bye, not because they felt inadequate to the task but simply because they loved Paul and would likely not see him again this side of heaven (Acts 20:36–38).

Lessons of the Third Journey

Third-journey leaders attract more high-quality apprentice leaders. The authority earned in a third-journey leader's life is easy to spot. Third-journey leaders have a confidence and a perspective that is attractive and empowering at the same time. These leaders are trusted, too. Emerging leaders do not feel as if they are being used for the mentor's project—actually, quite the opposite. They feel that their own success is of more value than the mentor's. Third-journey leaders have proved that they are good stewards of God's emerging leaders, and that is why God trusts third-journey leaders with His greatest resources.

Third-journey leaders have an expanding influence because others take their messages farther than the leaders could themselves. The message of the third-journey leader multiplies into the lives of others, through these leaders' apprentices and writings.

Although third-journey leaders may find they are doing less ministry work and are more focused, leaders at this stage are actually accomplishing more through the multiplication of new leadership. This journey, while not lacking in hard work and difficult trials, often sees production well beyond the one-to-one ratio of effort to result. The amount of well-focused effort seems to multiply its fruitfulness exponentially.

Third-journey leaders carry with them an increased spiritual authority that can come only from the hardships experienced in previous journeys.

This is the payoff for enduring the pain of learning in all the struggles of earlier adventures. You can't buy this authority with any currency other than sweat, blood, and tears. It is evident to everyone. People without authority who try to mimic a third-journey leader's methods will discover less than stellar results. Third-journey leaders' styles or methods cannot be mimicked to obtain third-journey results. This is not to say that you shouldn't learn from the third-journey leader's methods, but you must earn your own authority to see the same kind of fruit. It is not just skills and a ministry assignment that converge; it is one's maturity and character as well, which cannot be gained through shortcuts.

The work of the third journey was dynamic and powerful, and it spread quickly across an entire region. People were delivered from darkness into light. They left behind their old lives and became agents of the new life. Paul mentored the new converts in an on-the-job style, within the normal ebb and flow of life, so that they could take what they had learned to any place God called them to.

As a leader, have you reproduced yourself? If you were removed from your own ministry environment, what would remain? Are the people you trained leaving their old ways, taking up the cross, and bearing the Gospel to other people and places? Are you more concerned for the success of the people you have mentored than for your own success? Will the influence of your own life go beyond the driving distance to your church, or beyond your eulogy?

If these questions are a challenge for you, then perhaps you are still working your way through an earlier journey. I would estimate that most leaders in America are still at the first- or second-journey level; otherwise we would see far more reproduction of disciples, leaders, and churches.

Those who have blossomed to become third-journey leaders have come to experience a whole new level of fruitfulness. But there is still one more journey that can bring the most success. Paul's fourth journey was his most significant.

A bust of Nero found in the ancient city of Corinth.

6

The Fourth Journey
All Roads Lead to Rome

Success is not to be pursued; it is to be
attracted by the person you become.
—Jim Rohn

Now I want you to know, brethren, that my circumstances have
turned out for the greater progress of the Gospel.
—the apostle Paul describing his fourth journey (Philippians 1:12)

WE DO NOT USUALLY CONSIDER Paul's Roman imprisonment as a missionary journey, but I assure you, Paul did. He had intended to go to Rome (Romans 1:14–16), and on this trip the empire covered the cost of getting there. What is really surprising is that Paul considered this to be his most effective missionary journey, even though he spent almost all of the time locked up.

When he wrote to the Philippians while under house arrest in Rome, Paul explained that in this situation he was turning out to be more effective in proclaiming the Gospel around the world than when he had been free to travel (Philippians 1:12). Let the significance of this statement sink in a bit. Paul was saying that his being in prison was actually having a greater Gospel impact than he had been able to have when he could travel and preach the Gospel anywhere he wanted. How was that possible?

The impact of Paul's previous journeys had been local, for the most part, either when he was starting churches in particular locations or spreading the Gospel over an entire region, as happened on the third journey, in Asia. Paul's fourth journey, which landed him in the capital of the Roman Empire, would extend the Gospel's influence to the whole world.

Later, looking back on this journey Paul described it this way:

> At my first defense [before Caesar in Rome, on this fourth journey]
> no one supported me, but all deserted me; may it not be counted
> against them. But the Lord stood with me and strengthened me,
> so that through me the proclamation might be fully accomplished,
> and that all the Gentiles might hear; and I was rescued out of the
> lion's mouth.[1]

"All the Gentiles" was quite an ambitious missionary journey! The phrase refers to everyone on the planet who was not Jewish. How did Paul accomplish so much while being confined to a cell, a ship, and an apartment? That is exactly what this chapter will unpack.

Paul's Story: The Fourth Journey

By the end of the third journey, Paul had experienced much. He had instigated a movement of God that spread rapidly across all of Asia, to the point where every person who lived there heard the message of God. He had fought off wild beasts. He had engaged in spiritual battle with the devil himself. He had preached the Gospel to brand new places in Illyricum and had met with many of the churches he had started in previous journeys. He had escaped plots of assassination and recruited a growing team of Gentile Christian leaders. He had collected a large gift to present to the Jerusalem church. All of this was preparation for his greatest missionary journey of all, but one that would have a surprising way of coming to fruition.

There is a sense that Paul's fourth journey began during his return from his third journey. A shift from his normal pattern on this return trip was that he did not return to Antioch, as he had done with each of the other journeys, but only to Jerusalem. The stages of our life's maturity do not always follow the boundaries of well-defined ministry assignments. When you make the transition to another role or location, that doesn't necessarily mean that you are moving into another stage of ministry maturity. Paul's journeys certainly seem to be almost perfect overlaid by Clinton's phases of spiritual maturity, but that is not to be expected for most people. Nevertheless, the characteristics demonstrated by each of Paul's journeys are fairly common.

Luke uses familiar language to describe Paul's pilgrimage. He says, "Paul purposed in the Spirit to go to Jerusalem" (Acts 19:21). This is very reminiscent of Luke's description of Jesus, when he described

Him as "determined to go to Jerusalem" (Luke 9:51). The entire time Paul was traveling to Jerusalem, he was given prophetic warnings of what would happen to him there. Jesus also was well aware of the hardships that were awaiting him at the same destination.

Even though it is clear that the Holy Spirit was speaking about the bonds and imprisonment that awaited Paul, the message was not necessarily that he should not go. Since Paul already had "purposed in the Holy Spirit" to go, it was simply an opportunity to count the cost of following Christ—which he did, emphatically so, to the point where he loudly lamented, "What are you doing, weeping and breaking my heart? For I am ready not only to be bound, but even to die at Jerusalem for the name of the Lord Jesus" (Acts 21:13).

Like Jesus, Paul would face his destiny in Jerusalem, where the religious Jewish leaders there turned him over to the Gentiles for prosecution. Paul did not know a lot more than that about what would happen, but he did know that Jesus had told him he would speak before kings and rulers (Acts 9:15). This revelation gave him a reckless confidence in what he was to do, and so, in spite of all the prophetic warnings, he pressed on with his band of representatives from the churches of the Gentile world. Some interpretations of his actions have Paul disobeying the Holy Spirit on this return trip, but I think he was simply counting the cost of obedience and rising to the call. The severity of our testing increases with the depth of our maturity (1 Corinthians 10:13). It is doubtful that Paul would have received such a test of his obedience on earlier journeys, but at this point in his life he was equipped to face multiple prophetic warnings from spirit-filled prophets and still maintain his purpose. He passed this test. It is what he did once he arrived in Jerusalem that I believe is questionable.

When Paul finally arrived in Jerusalem, he and his companions met with the elders of the Jerusalem church to present the gifts they had brought. The mother of all churches had gone through some dramatic changes, however, and most of them were not good.

Earlier, it had been remarkable that many of the Judaic priests in Jerusalem had become followers of the Way (Acts 6:7). This was good news, of course, but I believe it brought a stauncher legalistic bent to the church as well. Although these leaders could agree that Jesus was the promised Messiah, they had no intention of dropping their own Jewish traditions, which unfortunately included a works-based righteousness. The church in Jerusalem became a more acceptable thing in the Judaic world. Paul, however, was not accepted.

Even in the early days of the church's life there was an undercurrent of religious bigotry that was never really addressed but simply accommodated (Acts 6:1). To be fair, this bigotry had been inherited and was the product of centuries of cultural persuasion, and it was based on what would clearly be seen as wicked and immoral practices. The influx of priests, highly invested in and committed to the temple and its traditional laws, magnified the spiritual disease that plagued the Jerusalem church.

It is far easier, in retrospect, to delineate some of these issues clearly, but at the time there was much confusion. Nevertheless, even today there is much debate, and so imagine how muddy the water was during Paul's day. Realize that at this point little of the New Testament had been written; the church was just beginning, and suddenly Gentiles were responding to the Gospel with obvious signs and wonders.

Some of the underlying questions that may have been burning up the oxygen in the room were these:[2]

> Were Gentiles to become Jews when they chose to follow the Messiah and obey all of the Torah?
>
> Were Gentile followers to become part of Israel or not?
>
> Was circumcision necessary to becoming part of "the faith" (which was Jewish in the eyes of the Jerusalem church)?
>
> Was Christianity a new faith or simply a sect of Judaism?
>
> Were Jews to stop living as Jews because of the Gospel?
>
> How much of the Torah was a Jew to live by, and how much was no longer relevant because of the Messiah and the salvation He brought?
>
> How did the Torah work to effectively sanctify a believer?
>
> Which parts of the oral traditions were true, and which were to be rejected?
>
> What role did the temple, sacrifices, and rituals play in the life of a follower of Jesus? Were there now two ways to be sanctified in Christ—the Jewish and the Gentile?

Imagine how hard it would have been to accept Paul's teaching, which was from personal revelation (Galatians 1:11–12), as against centuries of Holy Scripture and the traditions of God's leaders! Paul became a lightning rod in this struggle.

The many Judaic priests who had become part of the Jerusalem church probably felt that they had sure answers for all these questions. Even for those who were willing to ignore the Gentile churches, there was no way that God's chosen people were to stop being Jewish, or that the Torah was to be set aside. The Messiah came to fulfill the law, not to replace it.

The Torah, as they understood it, was universal, eternal, and necessary for life and godliness. For many, written law and oral law were hard to separate; Peter himself struggled with this for many years.[3] Some of the hateful views of the Gentiles that were so prevalent in Judaism seeped into the Jerusalem church and festered there. Paul's work and reputation became an incendiary factor in this bigotry, and a highly volatile environment was ignited when he arrived.

At this time the twelve apostles (the "sent ones") had gone on their various missions around the world, leaving behind the elders of the Jerusalem church, including its leader, James, the Lord's half-brother. James appears to have been balanced in his own views but was also fighting an uphill battle in trying to keep this church together and healthy. Luke tells us that there were many in the Jerusalem church who were said to be "zealous for the law," and who had heard and believed many unkind rumors about Paul. The rumors claimed that Paul was actually teaching Jews to stop being Jewish and to cease upholding the customs that had been taught to them in Mosaic law.[4] This was a lie, of course, fabricated by Paul's enemies, but a lie that is believed is very influential, especially in the mouths of people looking for an object of their scorn.

This presented James and the Jerusalem leaders with a quandary. How could they receive a financial gift from someone many of their people considered to be an enemy of the people of God? How could they appease this ugliness in a church already compromised in so many ways? They developed a plan that, I believe, involved some compromise on Paul's part. They asked him to sponsor four Jewish Christians who were completing an expensive purification vow. This had become a common practice and a way for wealthier people to participate in the process without needing to actually fulfill the vows themselves. The reasoning was that if people saw Paul upholding the Jewish customs, they might realize that the rumors were untrue.

It is easy to miss how significant this decision was for Paul. He must have felt conflicted about being asked to compromise on all that he had fought for. Certainly he saw himself as Jewish, and that was part of being Jewish. But Paul—in the end, to those under the law—became as under the law so that he might win those who were under the law (1 Corinthians 9:20). There are many commentators who view this as an easy decision that involved no compromise at all. I am not so certain.

This seven-day Nazarite process would have required Paul to be ceremonially cleansed, partly from having been in the presence of the "unclean" Gentiles. Given his long years of labor and fellowship with the Gentiles, I imagine this was a very difficult experience for Paul.

This part of the compromise cost him the most. I believe it would have gone against Paul's heart, the Spirit's leading, and even the truth revealed by God himself—that what God has cleansed can no longer be considered unclean (Acts 10:15). Certainly Paul could have changed its meaning in his own mind, but it communicated a message to the rest of the world that was exactly what he had spent his life refuting. Is this not a mistake similar to the one Peter made when he separated himself from eating with the unclean Gentile Christians (Galatians 2:11–14)?

The rest of the affair is easily summed up as a symbolic act accompanied by an underlying spiritual devotion. There is nothing so damaging about this. Expressing a personal vow in worship and devotion is not bad; Paul had done that himself earlier, without any compromise (Acts 18:18).

For us, this may be the low point of Paul's story. It is helpful, however, to realize that even a leader on a fourth journey can make his or her biggest mistake. Do not assume that because you are mature and have paid the price to be more seasoned, you are incapable of making a poor choice in the heat of a precarious moment. It also shows us that there is forgiveness and redemption for mistakes. One can finish well even with a mistake or two along the way.

It is important to note at this point that there are a large number of scholars who would disagree with my take on this choice of Paul's, and so I want to speak with much reserve about it. It is entirely possible that Paul had no hesitation in the act and saw it simply as personal devotion to Yahweh and as a chance to reach out to those "under the Law." He does later state to the Sanhedrin in Jerusalem, "I have lived my life with a perfectly good conscience before God up to this day" (Acts 23:1). If you do not hold to my point of view on this, you are in good company, and I am not dogmatically defending my position but merely presenting it as the option that I favor.

Whether or not you believe that Paul acted wrongly, we can all agree that his action accomplished next to nothing. It did not further his spiritual sanctification. It did not appease the legalistic Christians. It did not keep him from being attacked or imprisoned. It was not this vow that pleased Jesus but rather his uncompromising stance before the Sanhedrin (Acts 23:11). It did, however, give four men a chance to take an expensive vow that they couldn't afford on their own, and so I guess there was some good that came of it.

Near the end of the week, when it seemed that everything might turn out well, all hell broke lose. Some Jews from Asia, the place where Paul had experienced his greatest struggle and known his greatest fruitfulness, rose up and accused him of defiling the temple, and they told other poisonous lies. The crowds seem always to be easily agitated, and soon a violent mob seized Paul and threatened to kill him. But God had mercy and brought a cohort of Roman soldiers to rescue Paul, sparing his life and preventing a riot from occurring. From this point on in this journey, Paul would be imprisoned.

Calm Assurance in Chaotic Direction

The Roman commander who seized Paul literally had to have him carried away from the vicious mob that was ready to kill him. Ever the opportunist, Paul asked for permission to address the crowd. Luke, for whatever reason, goes out of his way to show how kind and accommodating the Roman soldiers were to Paul on this journey. At almost every turn, they showed him respect and granted him privileges above and beyond what would have been his due as a prisoner. Therefore, even this strange request of Paul's was granted. In this tense scene, Paul exhibited his artful use of language. He spoke to the Romans in excellent Greek, and he spoke to the Jews in perfect Aramaic. In both cases, his masterful use of the language took his listeners by surprise.

Bloodied and sore from being beaten, and now held in bondage, Paul spoke to the crowd from the steps of the Roman barracks, explaining his true heart to the very people who had attempted to tear him to pieces just moments earlier. In love, he preached the Gospel to those who hated him. He started by identifying with his audience in their zeal for the law. In fact, he told them how he had gone further than they had in his earlier pursuit of heretics, before Christ interrupted his journey to Damascus over twenty years before.

As he preached, he spoke about his own true cleansing of sins and baptism, perhaps implying that this religious ritual he had just attempted was all the more useless. Perhaps at this moment he was speaking as much to himself as to the crowd. Emboldened, he went even further and spoke of Jesus' call to him to bring the Gospel to the Gentiles. That was intolerable to the mob, which began to shout that he was not fit to live. But not only did Paul literally turn the other cheek and pray for those who persecuted him, he also stood up to their bigotry with boldness. This was a moment of redemption for Paul. Later, Jesus would tell him that because he had stood so boldly before the Jews, he would now be sent to Rome to stand before Caesar himself (Acts 23:11).

This time, when questioned by Roman soldiers, Paul was quick to pull out his Roman citizenship credentials before the soldiers could scourge him. Then he was brought before the Sanhedrin, and there he squared off against the high priest. Throughout this proceeding, Paul demonstrated a depth of understanding regarding all the subtleties of what was involved with this group of men, and he used this to his advantage in an impossible situation. Ananias, the high priest, ordered Paul to be struck on the mouth, supposedly for lying. Paul knew this was illegal and responded with authority, calling Ananias a whitewashed wall (of a tomb)! People in the council were shocked, asking, "Is that any way to speak to the high priest?" Paul acknowledged that he should not speak evil of a ruler, and he said he didn't know that Ananias was the high priest. That may have been true, but it may also have been a subtly sarcastic way of saying, "There is nothing about this man that indicates he is in any way suited to be high priest."

From about 170 B.C. on, the high priests were no longer descendants of Aaron but were actually appointed by Roman leaders. Ananias, the son of Seth, was appointed high priest by Quirinius, the governor of Syria, in 6 A.D. From that point on, he and his family ruled the Sanhedrin for fifty-plus years, with five sons, a son in law (Caiaphas), and a grandson all taking turns. That succession included this Annaias, who ordered Paul to be struck (Acts 23).[5] Flavius Josephus, in his *Antiquities of the Jews,* says about the family of Annaias: "Now the report goes, that this elder Ananus proved to be a most fortunate man; for he had five sons, who all performed the office of high priest to God, and he had himself enjoyed that dignity a long time formerly, which had never happened to any other of the high priests."[6] It may very well be that Paul was exposing this injustice by saying, "I was not aware, brethren, that he was high priest; for it is written, 'you shall not speak evil of a ruler of your people.'"

Normally, it would have been very clear who was the high priest in such a proceeding, and Paul was more than acquainted with the nuances of the Sanhedrin. There would have been many signals to indicate which of the men was in charge. Commentators differ on whether Paul was sincere or sarcastic in this remark; perhaps he was a little of both. Maybe he was assuming that some would think it a sincere comment and not bring any more physical discipline upon him, and at the same time he may have been making a sly comment with his tongue firmly in his cheek. He may have been fooling the foolish and doing so with some internal laughter. This episode reveals, in colorful fashion, the legalism that Paul was constantly fighting against. It was not obedience to Mosaic law that was at issue in this context, for Paul not only quoted it but also used it to attack the man who ordered him to be slapped. And then he immediately quoted it again with respect to not speaking evil of one's leaders.

It was the oral tradition, which had become law, that had corrupted the leaders and was being used to keep the people oppressed. This is what Jesus was also constantly countering.

Realizing that no good could come of this meeting, Paul declared himself a Pharisee who was on trial for standing up for the hope of the resurrection of the dead (which is true). Since this was a doctrinal difference between the Pharisees and the Sadducees, Paul cleverly distracted the council and got himself out of a precarious place. The commander ordered him removed from the bickering group.

On the next night, Jesus appeared, standing beside him, and said: "Take courage; for as you have solemnly witnessed to My case at Jerusalem, so you must witness at Rome also." How special this moment must have been to Paul! It was encouragement, enlightenment, empowerment, redemption, and a commissioning, all in one simple sentence! Paul was suffering from heinous acts of injustice—lies and fabrications had gotten him arrested without righteous cause. He was being tried on the basis of these accusations, yet it was Jesus' case, and Paul was merely a witness in the trial. I think sometimes we are a little too full of ourselves at these moments. We feel that we are the victims, and Jesus is just our comforter. Jesus' words reveal that this is not the way it is. Here, Jesus was the one under attack. Let us all remember that it is not our own reputations that are at stake in the missions to which we are called. It is His. The successes and the setbacks are His. It is His rejection, His reception—not ours.

These words from Jesus must have taken Paul back thirty years, to his vision on the road to Damascus, when he had been the one attacking Jesus. How far he had come! What a difference Jesus had made in his life! And his life was not over. He was to go finally to Rome! He would speak about the risen Lord to kings and rulers. Jesus can say much in just a few words. His word is powerful on so many levels simultaneously.

No sooner had Jesus spoken these words to Paul than his nephew happened to hear of an assassination plot against him. Such plots are not usually broadcast, and so God's hand was certainly evident. Immediately wheels were set in motion to bring Paul to preach the Gospel to the emperor of the world, because Jesus had said he should.

Success Without Trying

Paul was held captive for two years, first by Felix, a former slave who had become a Roman ruler, and then by Porcius Festus, who succeeded Felix. The leaders of the Jews in Jerusalem, who were still obsessed with killing Paul, appealed to Festus and requested that Paul be transferred to Jerusalem for trial, but in fact the plan was to ambush him along the way. With that, Paul appealed to be allowed to appear before Caesar, which was his right as a Roman citizen. Festus granted his request.

As it turned out, King Agrippa and his wife, Bernice, had come to Caesarea to welcome Festus. When Festus told them about Paul, Agrippa asked to hear from Paul. Paul boldly preached the Gospel to them and was quite persuasive. They could find no reason for Paul to be punished or even imprisoned, but since he had appealed to Caesar, he was sent on his way to Rome. Jesus' plan for Paul would not be thwarted.

When Paul set sail for Rome, Luke and Aristarchus, a Macedonian from Thessalonica, were with him. It is assumed that they would have had to become slaves of Paul in order to join him on this voyage. Perhaps this is true, and it may explain how Luke was able to be with Paul even in a dungeon, when Paul was facing execution (2 Timothy 4:11). Others speculate that Luke was on board as a ship's doctor. Either way, Luke doesn't tell us; he only informs us that these two apprentices joined Paul on the voyage, which first set off to Crete.

The harsh winds from the north were against them, and despite Paul's warnings, the centurion in charge of the ship insisted that they leave Crete even though winter was approaching. This would have been risky in a large ship that was steered clumsily with side oars, rather than a rudder, and that had a single large sail hoisted up on one mast. Without sextant or compass, they would have had to rely on the stars, and so the storm clouds brought multiple problems.

The violent north winds blew them off course, and the storms prevented them from knowing their whereabouts. They eventually began to lose hope. They took every measure possible to spare the ship and its passengers, but they were lost at sea and feared shipwreck on the rugged shores of North Africa.

In this scenario, something remarkable happened. Paul, a prisoner, rose to take charge. Aside from the fact that he was a very seasoned traveler who had already been shipwrecked three times before, he also had boldness and insight beyond anything the other men had encountered. Therefore, they not only listened to him but also did all they could to spare the lives of Paul, his companions, and even the rest of the prisoners with them. On the last evening of this ordeal, Paul told them to eat, and he broke bread with them. The language Luke uses is very reminiscent of the language used to describe a Eucharist. I believe that Paul took advantage of this moment to present the Gospel to these men they had all come to know so well in the midst of great adversity. The next day, they ran onto a sandbar off an unknown island, just as the Lord had promised Paul through an angelic messenger. All 276 passengers made it to the island of Malta.

Paul, like Jesus, was always a servant and willing to work, and once they were ashore, he began gathering sticks for a fire, since they were trying to warm up. A hibernating viper was aroused by the fire. It struck Paul on the hand and then hung there for all to see. Jesus had told Paul that he must appear before Caesar in Rome, and so, with a flick of the wrist and not a second thought, Paul disposed of the snake.[7] The native people assumed that he was evil and would die, but when there was no sign that the snakebite had hurt Paul, they thought he was a god.

They wintered among the people of Malta, whose leader was Publius. The leader's father was suffering from intense dysentery, and Paul healed him and many others as well. When spring arrived, three months later, they resumed their voyage to Rome, amply supplied by the hospitable islanders, who were grateful for all Paul had given them.

The rest of the voyage was without incident. Paul was greeted in Rome by a great delegation of Christ followers to honor him. Imagine what the Roman soldiers who had transported this prisoner must have thought of such a greeting. But perhaps by now they had seen enough to know why this man was so beloved.

Paul preached the Gospel first to the Roman Jews, as was always his pattern. They had not yet heard of him from Jerusalem. After a short time, however, some were convinced, whereas others rejected his message, as had so often been the case before.

Paul stayed in Rome for two years, living in rented quarters under house arrest, in the constant presence of a soldier who was guarding him. He was given visitation privileges, and so people were coming and learning from him all the time. The apartment must have been much more comfortable than a cell, but he had to pay the rent, even though he could not leave the apartment to work. Nevertheless, with so many people alongside him, he was not concerned about such things. The Philippian church even sent Epaphroditus with a gift package to help with his financial needs (Philippians 4:10–19).

On his fourth journey, Paul unleashed his most powerful Gospel work to date, but he couldn't even leave his apartment. Most of us, if we faced the same restraints, would give up on changing the world. We would have every excuse to just pass the time waiting for release. Perhaps some of us with more passionate drive would devote the time to reading or writing, but we would likely lose the hope of reaching the lost and starting churches. Paul did not.

The saying that all roads lead to Rome derives from the fact that the Romans invented the road and established roads all over the world to connect their vast empire and its trade routes. Thus, in a real sense, Paul was planted in the capital of the world, where paths of influence stretched out in every direction. His apartment became a global headquarters for a Jesus movement that would alter the known world.

Expansion of the Gospel During Paul's Fourth Journey

Today, with computers, the Internet, television, and telephones, it is feasible for someone to have an impact on the world and never leave his home, but how did Paul do it back then? Here are seven ways that Paul was able to make such a global impact on his fourth journey:

1. His legal appeal itself brought his message to key people, such as Felix and Drusilla, Festus, King Agrippa, and Bernice, and eventually even to Nero himself. In fact, it seems as if Paul just kept gaining more and more influence over more and more superior rulers. He went from prefects to regional kings to eventually preaching the Gospel to the emperor of the world.

2. Paul planted the first church of Malta on his way to Rome. He did not even know that such an island existed, and so he hadn't planned on starting a church there. But the Lord of the harvest knew, and it was in His plan. Paul started churches sometimes with only two or three weeks in a place, and so, given his three months on Malta, he probably reached the entire island.

3. Paul's reputation attracted many people to come and hear his message in his rented quarters. He must have had a large apartment, with room for many people. Not only did he have his own team staying with him frequently, he also could entertain many other people as well.

4. Paul's incarceration allowed him to write four epistles that would carry his message throughout the world and across time. While he was in Rome, Paul penned the four letters commonly called the prison epistles: Ephesians, Philippians, Colossians, and Philemon. Paul was the apostle to the Gentiles, and in a very real sense he still is. We are still learning from this apostle who changed the world forever by releasing the good news to the Gentile world.

5. One sure way of spreading the church is to take out her leaders, as has been shown throughout church history. Wherever pastors have been killed or locked up, the church has prospered. I'm not sure what that says about our leadership, but it's not just about us, since this was true

even in Paul's time. His being locked up provoked others to take up his mission because it was assumed that he no longer could do it (Philippians 1:14–18).

6. During his stay in Rome, Paul had access to lost people that the church could never have reached otherwise. That sounds strange. What people would he have had access to if he couldn't leave his own apartment? Well, you might say he had a captive audience. All day, every day, there was a Roman soldier no more than a couple of steps from him. The Romans were outstanding military strategists. They knew that to keep a soldier alert on his watch, it was necessary to rotate assignments. One day a guard would be beside Paul, receiving the life of Jesus, and the next day he might be protecting the emperor's daughter. While he was under house arrest, Paul wrote to the Philippians that all who were in Christ in Rome sent their greetings, especially those of Caesar's own household (Philippians 1:13–14; Acts 28:16; Philemon 4:22). The Gospel had spread virally and even infiltrated the palace, into Nero's own *oikos*. Legend has it that some of Nero's own family members were executed for following Christ. The soldiers who guarded Paul took the Gospel message to other places as well, all over the empire. They were missionaries sent by and paid for by Rome. I like to think that Paul took advantage of his writing a letter to the Ephesians to open a conversation about the Gospel when a new soldier came on duty to watch him. I imagine him busy writing a letter, then stopping, looking to one side, then writing a little more: "Belt of truth." Then he would look back at the soldier again and go immediately back to writing: "Helmet of salvation." He would continue, giving the soldier another look, and then write more. Eventually the soldier probably asked him what he was writing. I imagine Paul saying, "I am describing the most powerful soldier in the world today." The soldier was probably flattered and stood more upright with a look of pride. Paul would shake his head, and say, "Oh, it's not you. I'm just using you as a model. This soldier can actually fight off evil spirits of all kinds and not lose ground." I imagine that Paul's guard was so intrigued that he eventually enlisted in the kind of army Paul was describing.

7. Paul was always mentoring new leaders and sending them out to reproduce his ministry and multiply his influence around the world. Both Acts and the prison epistles mention many people who were with Paul during his imprisonment, including Epaphroditus, Timothy, Luke, Mark, Demas, Aristarchus, Jesus (called Justus), Epaphras, Tychicus, and

Onesimus. We can assume that there were even more who were not mentioned, including the soldiers. These disciples of Jesus, empowered and mentored by Paul, would strike out across the world on the roads radiating from Rome to do works like those that Paul had done on his earlier journeys.

Paul reproduced himself. Where once there was only one team, made up of Barnabas and Saul, now there were multiple teams being sent off all over the world. This is how Paul could say, "Through me the proclamation might be fully accomplished, and all the Gentiles might hear" (2 Timothy 4:17).

Luke's narrative ends with Paul's imprisonment. This was the end of the book of Acts, but not the end of Paul's journeys, and certainly not the end of the work that is chronicled in Acts.

Lessons of the Fourth Journey

Most Christian leaders will never get to the fourth journey. Most will plateau, if they don't die during an earlier journey. But God is faithful and usually provides a small handful of such leaders for every generation.

The fourth-journey leader cares less about daily provisions than he or she used to. Fourth-journey leaders no longer write support letters or wonder about how they will pay the rent. They have matured enough to learn the secret of contented faith that keeps them calm under any and all pressures. Paul wrote from his rented quarters to the Philippians that he had learned the secret of contentedness in any circumstance that God might grant him. He thanked them for their financial gift but also told them he didn't need it. He was more excited about the blessing that giving had brought to them than about what it had brought to him. He knew God had called him to Rome, and so it was up to God to get him there, which He did. When God places the order, He pays the bill.

The fourth-journey leader's reputation can increase even in the eyes of the world's leaders. Because Paul faithfully pursued Christ, eventually he had audiences with governors, kings, and the emperor. Some even sought his counsel while he was under their incarceration (Acts 24:24–26).

The fourth journey has more expansive influence, beyond what expectations or circumstances would dictate. On his third journey, Paul took three years to reach a single region of Asia, and he was free not only to teach in the school of Tyrannus but also to move about from house to house. On this trip, his most effective time was only two years, and he was confined to his apartment, and yet he was able to reach the whole

Gentile world because others took his message for him. By doing less, he did more, which is a fourth-journey characteristic.

The fourth journey is when leaders often expand their written influence so that countless others benefit from their experience and maturity. Some leaders get absorbed with writing too soon, and the learning ends as soon as they become experts. The great writers continue growing and learning, and fourth-journey leaders write books that are read for generations, not simply for the moment. The authority behind their words comes from the hard-won lessons of enduring all the previous journeys.

Fourth-journey leaders no longer get stressed over their work. By this time, these leaders have become comfortable in their skin, and they allow the work to flow naturally from the people they have become. They find success without really trying, simply by being content in Christ and letting the work come to them in whatever fashion it may. They have confidence that God will do the work that He always intended, and they do not feel compelled to make it happen.

The fourth-journey leader still faces life tests and continues to experience character growth. The battles we face against the world, the flesh, and the devil will last throughout our lifetimes. Those who make it to the fourth journey are not immune to the challenges of character trials. In fact, often the temptations of a fourth-journey leader may be subtler but all the more intense. Paul was attacked by a mob, falsely accused, threatened with death, shipwrecked, and incarcerated. It was on this journey that Paul might have committed his greatest mistake. Redemption is as readily available to fourth-journey leaders as to any others.

At the risk of putting something in print that I may later regret, I will say that we have been blessed with a couple of fourth-journey leaders in our world today. One is passing on and another is just emerging.

Billy Graham has been on a fourth journey for some time. In one way or another, he has exhibited all the qualities I've just mentioned. He has continued to grow in his spiritual life. Presidents and kings have sought his counsel. His influence has spread, and in his later years he has invested in future evangelists who will carry on after he has gone.

I believe that Rick Warren is another such leader, one just recently stepping into his fourth journey. On his first journey, Rick influenced south Orange County. Then his influence went national with *The Purpose-Driven Church* and *Forty Days of Purpose*. Now he is stepping into new authority, and his influence is spreading on a global scale with what he is calling his PEACE Plan. Presidents seek his counsel and blessing in much the same way as they have done with Graham. Rick's first books are good and they have sold well, but *The Purpose-Driven Life* carries a weight that the others do not. I find that book nearly omnipresent, seemingly in every room I walk into. This success cannot be attributed to a great marketing campaign or a catchy title.

Rick and I have very different churches, and our gifts and callings have taken paths that seem to go in contrasting directions, but I have always found him to be a godly man of great faith, and I hope that one day I can be as faithful in my pursuit of our Lord. Rick is such a positive person that he would never be found complaining. His ministry and his life may seem charmed and blessed beyond most, but I know that he has had his fair share of deep and heartfelt struggles, which have fortified his character so that his influence has been able to continue expanding on a global scale without changing who he is. For every remarkable blessing and success, he has had a personal challenge or grief.

I pray for Rick and ask God to continue to open doors of influence for him, and I would challenge others to do the same even if they would not do church the same way. I do not think it is his strategy or plans that have birthed such influence, it is actually the man that he has become. All of us, including Rick, would be mistaken to attribute the fruitfulness of his life to simply a sound strategic plan or even the strength of his personality. While he and I are very different in our philosophies of ministry, I do know that he loves Jesus more than life itself and has a deep abiding passion to see lost and broken people restored to their creator. I sincerely hope and pray that this journey of Rick's is his most fruitful, for his sake and ours.

Rick Warren and Billy Graham are examples of fourth-journey leaders from whom we can learn today because they are very public figures. Not all fourth-journey leaders are as well known, however. Many live lives of humble obscurity. I am convinced that the bones of some of the greatest heroes of God's kingdom lie in unmarked and unremarkable graves. Those heroes are unknown here and now, and they may never have been famous, but they will be greatly honored in the next life. Do not think that you have to become a celebrity to be a fourth-journey leader. And certainly do not think that real success is to become famous. Real success is to find out what God wants of you and to do it with faith, beyond any realistic expectation, to your last breath.

Onesimus, Lasting Fruit of the Fourth Journey

To demonstrate Paul's fourth-journey influence, I would like to take a closer look at Onesimus, one of the men mentioned as being with him in his Roman imprisonment, because I believe his story best illustrates what was going on in Paul's apartment. Much of what I am about to write is speculation based on the facts we do know from the New Testament accounts, but it does illustrate what I believe was happening while Paul was on this journey.

Onesimus had been born into slavery in Asia Minor. He wanted freedom more than anything else, even family, and so one day he had stolen from his master and run away. A runaway slave had no rights, and if caught he would have received a severe punishment, not only to teach him a lesson but also to set an example for others.

Wanting to start a new life, Onesimus decided that the best place to go and not be noticed was a big city. In a small town, he couldn't blend in and remain anonymous, but perhaps in Rome he could.

Once he was in Rome, he found that he was not free at all. He was afraid of being caught, and he was lonely because any close relationship was either built on lies or nonexistent. He could never trust someone enough to reveal who he really was. Finding decent work was difficult without any references or background.

Somehow he heard that the apostle Paul was in town and accepting visitors. He remembered the difference that Paul's message had made to his old master and was intrigued by the thought of meeting the apostle. One day Onesimus awoke in desperation, still longing for freedom, and decided that this day he would finally be free or he would be dead. I speculate that he made this decision because somehow he had chosen to walk into the presence of a Roman guard and spill his guts to Paul. This could have meant immediate seizure and punishment, perhaps even death. Nevertheless, he went.

Fortunately, on this day, the soldier guarding Paul had become a follower of Christ. Onesimus heard the Gospel and found true freedom and was immediately discipled by Paul, who put him to work right away. With new freedom, Onesimus found that he had a reason to live and serve, and so he became very useful to Paul. After some time of training, Paul realized that for Onesimus to develop further he would have to reconcile his past with his master, Philemon. Therefore, Paul wrote two letters, one to Philemon and one to the church that met in Colossae, in Philemon's home. He may have also included the Laodicean letter at this time as well, since Laodicea was a neighboring town. With the epistles packed in his bag, Onesimus embraced Paul and his companions and went on a long journey of his own.

When he came into familiar country, near Colossae, he awoke one morning and decided again that on this day he would be either free or dead, a decision that we all must learn to make on a daily basis. He was about to enter the home of his master and turn himself in.

I imagine that at the moment when the two came face to face, Onesimus handed the letters to his master and bowed very low to the ground. I see Philemon reading the letters and granting Onesimus his freedom. We can read about that in the second chapter of Philemon. Well, actually, there is no second chapter of the letter to Philemon. But the letter itself, by its very existence, does tell us something about Onesimus's freedom. If Philemon had chosen not to grant Onesimus his freedom, we can be confident that he would not have circulated the letter that today is included in the canon of the New Testament.

There is nothing more said about either Philemon or Onesimus in the Bible, but there is a historic document that mentions Onesimus. In a letter written by Ignatius of Antioch roughly thirty years after John wrote the book of Revelation to the Ephesian church and her sisters in Asia Minor, Onesimus is mentioned. This letter is illuminating for us on two levels. First, it answers a question for us about what became of Onesimus, and, second, it answers a question about what became of the Ephesian church.

The New Testament does not close with a good word about this highly influential church. Jesus has John write a letter to the church. He describes it as sound in its doctrine and intolerant of false apostles but says she has lost something of utmost importance—her first love. Jesus tells the church to repent or be removed from His presence. With that, the Bible ends its discussion of the Ephesian church.

Here are the words of Ignatius to the Ephesians sometime later:

> I gave a godly welcome to your church which has so endeared itself to us by reason of your upright nature, marked as it is by faith in Jesus Christ, our Savior, and by the love of Him. You are imitators of God; and it was God's blood that stirred you up once more to do the sort of thing you do naturally and have now done to perfection. . . . In God's name, therefore, I received your large congregation in the person of Onesimus, your bishop in this world, a man whose love is beyond words. My prayer is that you should love him in the Spirit of Jesus Christ and all be like him. Blessed is He who let you have such a bishop. You deserved it![8]

To judge from Ignatius's letter, the Ephesian church returned to her first love, and a new age of fruitfulness was born. Jesus once said that the one who is forgiven much, loves much. It took the influence of a man like Onesimus, who knew firsthand what forgiveness was all about, to stir this church up once more to the love of Christ. The little-known runaway slave not only found the freedom he so desperately wanted but also started on some journeys to significance that ended with his taking a leadership role in one of the most influential churches of the first century. The fruit of Paul's fourth journey was enduring in the lives of the people he mentored.

There was one more journey left for Paul, and it would become the capstone of his life. This is a journey that we all must make, but we do not all make it as well as Paul did.

The Mamertine prison in Rome, where Paul spent his last days prior to execution and wrote 2 Timothy.

The Final Journey

Influence Beyond the Grave

> *In times of drastic change, it is the learners who*
> *inherit the future. The learned find themselves well*
> *equipped to live in a world that no longer exists.*
> —Eric Hoffer

> *But you [Timothy], be sober in all things, endure hardship,*
> *do the work of an evangelist, fulfill your ministry. For*
> *I am already being poured out as a drink offering, and the*
> *time of my departure has come.*
> —the apostle Paul at the end of his life (2 Timothy 4:5–6)

AT THE END OF THE GRUELING 26.2-MILE COURSE OF THE 1980 BOSTON MARATHON, a woman emerged into the glow of the finish line, smiling and waving to the cheers and the cameras. Cuban-born New Yorker Rosie Ruiz passed under the finish banner with a record time. To all appearances, she had bettered her own best time by more than twenty-five minutes and had finished a good two and a half minutes ahead of Jacqueline Gareau of Canada, the apparent runner-up. I say "apparent" because Ruiz was later discovered to have cheated. She had ducked out of the race at an earlier spot, caught a subway that took her to within a mile of the finish line, and reentered the race in front of Gareau, to steal the applause and the credit from the true winner.

In our own spiritual race, there are no shortcuts and there is no cheating. We either finish strong or we do not. Finishing well in our spiritual lives means pushing through pain and hardship. Paul did that, and he won his race. At the end of his life he could say with a clear conscience,

"I have fought the good fight, I have finished the course, I have kept the faith" (2 Timothy 4:7).

Paul's Last Journeys

We have very little insight into what happened after Paul's first Roman imprisonment, which occurs at the end of Acts. Nevertheless, we can piece some information together from the pastoral epistles and from other historical documents.

After his release from Rome, Paul may have gone to Spain, as he had indicated he intended to do (Romans 15:23–29). The first-century Christian leader Clement seems to indicate (1 Clement 5:6–7) that Paul preached as far as the limits of the West, which was likely Spain.[1]

Paul's time in the West could not have been long, since during this brief time he was also in Crete, initiating new works and leaving Titus there to complete them (Titus 1:5). From Crete, Paul and Timothy traveled toward Macedonia, but Timothy stayed in Ephesus to address some problems in the church (1 Timothy 1:3).

Paul went on to Macedonia and while there wrote 1Timothy and Titus. Paul spent a winter in Nicopolis (Titus 3:12) and it's likely that he was headed back to Ephesus when he was arrested in Troas (2 Timothy 4:13–15), probably betrayed by a man named Alexander.

A short time after he wrote to Titus, Paul was deserted by Demas, Titus, and Crescens, out of their love for the world (2 Timothy 4:10).[2] Perhaps Titus had a negative response to Paul's letter and left his post for that reason, but all we know is that Paul associates Titus with the statement about loving the present world. On his way to Rome, after his arrest in Troas, Paul must have stopped in Miletus and Corinth (2 Timothy 4:20), where some of his associates remained, for reasons far more favorable than those given for his separation from Demas, Titus, and Crescens.

His arrest landed him in a damp, cold dungeon in Rome, where he wrote his last letter, which we call 2 Timothy. This imprisonment was to be his last. In 67 A.D., Paul was beheaded.

After traveling 15,000 miles (8,700 by land), enduring four shipwrecks, starting churches in seven- or eight-people groups, writing fifteen letters that we know of (thirteen of which are in the New Testament), and enduring multiple imprisonments and uncounted beatings, he ended his life almost alone.[3] According to 2 Timothy, he spent his last days short on time (4:9), cold (4:13), lonely (4:11), rejected by his own spiritual children (1:15), abandoned by his sons in the faith (4:10), and betrayed by someone he trusted (4:14). Nevertheless, even though few stood with him in the end, he was a success (4: 6–8). My friend Bob Logan defines success as finding out what God wants you to do and doing it. If indeed that is success, then Paul finished quite well.

I visited Rome a few years ago with my eldest daughter, Heather, and we went to the Mamertine prison, also called Paul's prison, where Paul, at the end of his life, is believed to have written 2 Timothy.[4] We descended into the prison, and I could touch the ceiling with my head when I stood upright. Heather and I looked at each other in the prison's dim light, with the smell of mildew in our noses, and I realized that this was the very place where God had inspired one of my favorite books of the Bible. In this tiny space, Paul had agonized over his few remaining days and the lasting impact of his life. He had been here just hours before his execution, just hours before his soul was transferred into the light of God's eternal presence. It is in places like this prison that real heroes are found.

What a contrast with the Vatican, which we visited later the same day. Great riches of history adorned the Papal Palace and the rest of this religious city. The ceiling of the Sistine Chapel is too high to touch, but touching wouldn't have been permitted anyway—the chapel's ceiling is a masterpiece by Michelangelo.

Both sites, the Vatican and the Mamertine prison, impressed me deeply. Books of the Bible have also been written in places like the Vatican, but not as many as those written in dungeons by authors who were on the run in the wilderness, with posses breathing down their necks. My art background had drawn me to the Vatican, but my heart never left the cave of Paul's prison. Standing there, and trying to imagine Paul in that place at the end of such a fruitful life, changed me forever.

I couldn't help asking myself which of these two places I, as a Christian leader, would prefer. And I'm afraid that too many of us would choose the elegance and posh atmosphere of privilege over the cold, hard, unforgiving stone of a prison cell. But when I think about the leaders throughout history who have finished well, it seems to me that many of them have lived out their days in dark, marginalized locales. By contrast, we have taken to exalting the people who make the most money, are good-looking, and have the most fame, whether they are actors, musicians, or athletes, and regardless of their character. Nevertheless, the leaders with the greatest significance usually do not come from places of comfort, elegance, and privilege but from situations of pain, hardship, and great challenge. The leaders who finish strong are forged under pressure of great adversity, conviction, and challenge. May we all choose the dark cave of obscurity over the posh privilege of the Vatican.

Redefining Success for Leaders

Paul's influence is found even today; you're holding it in your hands right now. His writings and his life story have continued to influence millions of people. In fact, my own hope in writing this book has been that Christian leaders will strive to have the type of expanding influence that Paul had throughout his life, and that we will finish strong, as he did.

The greatest test of our success as leaders is not how many people come to our preaching conferences or buy our books. The real test of our leadership comes at the end of life, our final exam. How we end is perhaps the most important part of our lives. Paul took that test and passed it with flying colors. He became an example to Timothy, and to us.

At the end of his life, many had turned away from Paul. It is more than likely that he had been arrested one too many times, and so people began to doubt his character. There were many scoundrels who slandered his good name, and some people began to believe the slanders after hearing them so often. Other leaders were perhaps more popular or demanded greater audiences, but Paul was faithful and fruitful, and he finished well. The test of his greatness came long after his eulogy. The world that he lived in was changed for his having lived in it. We also have Paul's influence all over what we know and experience today as Christians. How many of us can claim greater fruitfulness through our absence than through our presence? We can even question whether we are successful if our success depends on our being present. All of us need a longer-range view of what success really is. I want my influence to go beyond the driving distance to my church, and beyond my eulogy. Paul had that kind of success.

It is not how many people buy our books in the first month but how many are still reading them seventy years later that determines our success as authors. It is not how well our children do in school today but how well they raise their own children decades later that determines our success as parents. Likewise, it is not how many people attend our churches today that determines our success as pastors but how many other pastors are left to lead the churches that remain when we have gone.

Why Some Do Not Finish Well

In *Organic Leadership* I stated that three things sum up success for the Christian—faithfulness, fruitfulness, and finishing well. According to J. Robert Clinton, however, about 70 percent of Christian leaders will not finish well.[5] That is alarming. Often when I am speaking to an audience,

I ask everybody to look to the left and then to the right, and I say that if Clinton's odds are accurate, only one leader in each unit of three will finish well.

Leaders become plateaued when they get sidetracked and stop maturing. There can be many reasons. They may have fallen victim to the lust of the flesh, the lust of the eyes, or the boastful pride of life and thereby compromised their spiritual values. They may have become hurt and hardened by the trials of life and, through a desire to no longer feel pain, may have moved to a status less conducive to struggle. Perhaps they have just grown weary of trying and have sought a more comfortable existence.

The following ten characteristics, mentioned in my book *Organic Leadership,* are those of plateaued leaders. Read through this list prayerfully and with introspection. If you feel that many of these qualities are reflective of your own spiritual life, then you may have become plateaued and may need to restart on your next journey to significance. Spiritually plateaued leaders . . .

1. *Avoid relationships of personal accountability.* These leaders are removed from people. They have a degree of separateness that keeps them unaccountable. Often, in fact, Christendom has reinforced such separation and tried to justify it as biblical, to the detriment of the church, the world, and especially to leaders themselves.

2. *Have infrequent personal application of God's word.* Many Christian leaders have pursued their own education only to the extent of becoming experts on the Bible. Once they become experts, it is easy for them to fall into the trap of thinking of themselves as people who have mastered a subject rather than as people who still have much to learn.

3. *Have seen joy, peace, and love replaced with envy and resentment.* One simply cannot manufacture godliness by modifying one's behavior to conform to Christ's ideals. The character that is to be evident in our lives is the fruit of having God's Spirit consuming our lives rather than the fruit of the works we carry out to demonstrate our spiritual conformity.

4. *Frequently look for greener pastures in other places.* It has become quite frequent for Christian leaders to blame their environment for the lack of fruitfulness in their ministry. This is a cheap but unfortunately common excuse. Others' success is usually also attributed to their being lucky enough to have landed in the right place at the right time. The consequences for leaders who think in this way is that they are always looking to land in a better place, where their ministry will be truly appreciated and their deserved success will finally come.

5. *More easily find faults in others than in themselves.* Plateaued leaders can find others' faults quickly, but introspection is a hard thing. These

leaders rarely evaluate themselves and are busy evaluating everyone else. This is certainly not a new phenomenon, by any means. Jesus humorously described such a leader as one who finds the speck in his brother's eye but does not notice the log protruding from his own (Matthew 7:3–5).

6. *Are burned out from lots of activity that has been substituted for intimacy with Christ.* It is most common to find that spiritually plateaued leaders are exhausted. It is not only because they value the sympathy that is evoked. One of the reasons for so much burnout is that these leaders are deceived into thinking that more effort and more activity are ways to gain closer access to and more blessings from God. This is a devastating lie from hell itself.

7. *Compromise ethical principles once held dear.* It is not uncommon to find that such leaders as I am describing have actually fallen deep into patterns of hidden sin. Using grace and liberty as an excuse, they continue to function publicly without regret or remorse, and behind closed doors they carry on dark practices.

8. *Stay within safe areas of expertise rather than branching out into new learning endeavors.* These leaders view themselves as experts rather than learners. Therefore, they have no intention of exploring new fields or breakthroughs in understanding. They are not on a growth trajectory. Instead, they stay in the same field and relay the same facts. These leaders continue to tell the same old stories from years past. There are some pastors who keep the same fifty-two sermons to repeat each year in new pastorates. The idea of learning something new is scary to them because it implies that they do not really have the expertise with which they identify themselves.

9. *Are teachers and experts more than learners.* These leaders talk more easily than they listen. In fact, they are easily offended by or uninterested in the instruction coming from others. Two words often heard from these leaders are "I know."

10. *Have reduced the Christian life to the rut of a routine.* Plateaued leaders are not moving forward. They have stabilized and are now in a holding pattern. As such, the Christian walk for these people means just continuing to carry on with the same old routine. Theirs is a static existence of maintaining what is rather than forging something that is not. For these leaders, the Christian life is just doing the right Christian things in the right Christian way. It is a life of a few *do's* and many *don'ts*.

Five Ways to Increase Your Chances of Finishing Well

J. Robert Clinton's research has yielded lots of helpful information about what goes into making a leader who finishes strong.[6] After all his study, he has identified the following five factors that enhance a leader's chances of finishing well:

1. *Perspective.* Leaders who finish well usually have a perspective that focuses their energies on ministry strengths over the course of their lives. Seeing the whole picture gives them the type of perspective that sees beyond the immediate and helps them invest in the long haul. It is common for such leaders to take stock regularly by asking, "What would be left if I were to die today?" This is not a morbid interest in death but a perspective on what it will take to finish well over a lifetime.

2. *Renewal.* These leaders enjoy repeated periods of spiritual renewal. It is not enough that these leaders have had experiences of renewal in the past. Leaders who finish well see life as a series of peak moments, connected by times they have had to pass through valleys. Many leaders who finish strong recognize this need in their life and intentionally schedule time alone with God for renewal. Such a time is not so much a vacation as a listening and waiting retreat. If even Jesus needed times such as these, how much more do you and I need them?

3. *Discipline.* Leaders who finish well have learned to discipline their spiritual formation. People don't just spontaneously enter a marathon and run it on the day of the race if they haven't invested the necessary time in training. Finishing well over the course of a lifetime is not accidental but intentional. If you do not choose to take the steps necessary to discipline your development, then it's more than likely that you will land among the two-thirds of leaders who do not finish well.

4. *Learning.* These leaders maintain a learning posture throughout life. There is an insatiable hunger to learn, an untamed curiosity, that carries them through. These are not the leaders who become experts and then never learn again. They enjoy branching out into new territory and discovering new things. It is easy to find older people who haven't grown or changed since they were young. It is rare to find the vitality of life that keeps people learning until they die, but that is what separates the winners from the losers in this race to finish well. The leaders who last are the leaders who learn.

5. *Mentoring.* Relationships are vital to life. Leaders who finish well recognize that such a feat does not come about without assistance. Leaders who finish well mentor others and are mentored themselves. They do not restrict themselves to a single mentor, as if one person can contain all that they need. They usually have many voices that speak into their lives and hold them accountable to what is truly important. We need mentoring in order to finish well. More than that, we need to mentor the next generation. The very definition of finishing well requires that we leave this planet in the care of the next generation of leaders. Unlike

the Dead Sea, which receives water from many tributaries but contributes to none and is therefore stagnant and dead, leaders who finish well are constantly growing because they are always giving and receiving.

Finish Well or Die Trying

In *Search & Rescue,* I tell a cautionary story that bears on the idea of a strong finish, and so I include it here as well.[7] In high school, I had the privilege of belonging to a very competitive swim team. We were good enough to win, and everyone expected that we would.

In our league we had just one other rival that could compete with us—the Westchester High team. Before the city finals, we faced this rival at the league finals. We were waiting to peak at the city championships, and so we had not prepared as well as we could have. And Westchester knew it, too, so the Westchester team had worked hard to peak here at the league finals, and to try to beat us. Our rivals on the Westchester team swam better than anyone had expected them to, and they went head to head with us through all the events. The league championship finally came down to the last race, the 200-yard freestyle relay.

Our team had a secret weapon—Zach. He was the fastest sprinter in the league. Unfortunately, however, he had injured his shoulder earlier in the season, and though he had worked hard to get back in shape and make up for lost time, he had missed many meets. And now, all the training he had been able to do since his injury was for this one moment.

Zach rose to the challenge. He dove in after the third leg of the relay, and he swam with no hesitation, no reservations, no thought at all except to touch the wall before his counterpart on the Westchester team. He gave it everything he had and moved clearly into first place. In the last few strokes, his shoulder popped out of its socket, but Zach swam through the pain and touched the wall first. Everyone in the stands was cheering, and the noise in the natatorium was so loud that my skin was vibrating.

We won! We won the relay, the meet, and the league championship. The year was ours. All the sacrifice and early-morning workouts had paid off. In one glorious moment of struggle and endurance, our team had pulled together and tasted victory. In the thrill of the moment, without thinking, one of my teammates, whose name I will not mention and will never forget, jumped into the water to embrace Zach and help lift him out of the pool. Unfortunately, however, one of the other teams had not yet finished the race, and so our team was automatically disqualified because of this simple, spontaneous act, lacking in forethought but full of the best intentions. I will never forget the sinking feeling that came over all of us as we began to realize what had happened. It spread across the spectators like a cold wave.

We lost! We lost the relay, the meet, and the league championship. Through one moment of thoughtless emotional reaction, our team was made to taste the bitterness of defeat and disgrace. All the sacrifice, all the hard work, and all the year's effort came down to a crashing defeat. Returning from the meet, I had never been on a quieter bus ride. The air seemed to have been sucked out of our lungs. We could barely breathe, let alone speak. Besides, we had nothing positive to say.

The analogy is obvious. What could be more disastrous than working hard all your life to finish well, only to be disqualified at the very end? But Paul was not disqualified. He finished a success, in every sense. He determined early in his life that he would finish well.

Eugene Peterson, who gave us *The Message,* has a book that takes its title, curiously, from a passage in *Beyond Good and Evil* by Friedrich Nietzsche, the famous atheist who declared that God is dead. The title of Peterson's book is *A Long Obedience in the Same Direction;* here are Nietzsche's words: "The essential thing 'in heaven and earth' is . . . that there should be a long obedience in the same direction; there thereby results, and has always resulted in the long run, something which has made life worth living."

Paul viewed his life as a great race. He wrote to the Corinthian church (1 Corinthians 9:24–27):

> Do you not know that those who run in a race all run, but only one receives the prize? Run in such a way that you may win. Everyone who competes in the games exercises self-control in all things. They then do it to receive a perishable wreath, but we an imperishable. Therefore I run in such a way, as not without aim; I box in such a way, as not beating the air; but I buffet my body and make it my slave, so that, after I have preached to others, I myself will not be disqualified.

We have seen that there is a price to pay if we want to finish well. That is probably the reason why so few do. We must make our minds up now to finish well if we hope to do so. Finishing well is no accident. And finishing well is not just something that happens at the end of life. It happens every day. We must choose today to finish well, and we must make the same choice every day. We must live as if every day were the last. Like Paul, we must decide today that we will finish well or die trying.

Appendix 1

An Estimated Chronology for the Journeys of Paul

YEAR	PAUL'S LIFE	ROMAN HISTORY
14–37 A.D.		Tiberius is emperor
30	Christ is crucified	
32	Stephen is stoned	
35	Paul is converted	
35–37	Paul is in Damascus and Arabia	
37	Paul visits Jerusalem and then visits Tarsus	
37–41		Galus (Caligula) is emperor
37–47	Paul is in Tarsus	
41–54		Claudius is emperor
46	Barnabas goes to Syria looking for Paul	
47	Paul is in Antioch teaching	
	Agabus prophesies of famine	
	Barnabas and Paul take famine relief to Jerusalem	
47–48	Paul makes his first missionary journey (Cyprus and Galatia)	
48	Paul returns to Antioch and reports to the church on his first journey	

49	Galatians is written	
	Jerusalem council is held, and letter is dispatched	
	Paul and Barnabas split	
49–53	Paul makes his second missionary journey (Macedonia/Achaia)	Claudius expels Jews from Rome
50	Paul has his Macedonian vision	
51	1 Thessalonians is written	
	Paul is in Corinth	
52	2 Thessalonians is written	
53	Paul returns to Jerusalem and Antioch	
53–57	Paul makes his third missionary journey (Asia and beyond)	
54–68		Nero is emperor
54	1 Corinthians is written	
56	2 Corinthians is written	
	Romans is written	
	Paul travels to Illyricum, Macedonia, and Greece	
	Paul stops in Asia on his way back to Jerusalem	
57–62	Paul makes his fourth missionary journey (Rome)	
57	Paul is in Jerusalem	
59	Paul is before Festus and Agrippa	
	Paul voyages to Rome	
60–62	Paul is under house arrest in Rome	
	Philippians, Ephesians, Colossians, and Philemon are written	

62	Paul is released and begins his last missionary work	
	1 Timothy is written	
	Titus is written	
64	Paul is arrested and brought back to Rome	Rome burns in the Great Fire
	2 Timothy is written	Nero begins persecution of Christians
66	Paul is executed under Nero	
68		Nero commits suicide
69		Vespian rises to emperor
70		Romans destroy the temple

Appendix 2

What Went Wrong with the Jerusalem Church?

THROUGHOUT THE HISTORY OF THE CHURCH, PEOPLE have longed to relive the experience of the first church as recounted in the book of Acts. In fact, as one attempt to relive that moment, an entire segment of Christendom—the Pentecostal segment—is named after the first day of the church. A great many churches have used the opening chapters of Acts as a guide to how they are to be structured, find purpose, and function. Of all the churches in the book of Acts, I personally believe the Jerusalem church to be the poorest model and the one we should be cautious about following.[1]

Of course there is much to learn in the opening chapters of Acts, and I would not discount the beauty and power evident there. The success of the church in Jerusalem is legendary, and I would not take anything away from it, but I would add that its success was short-lived and localized. Within just a few years the church had hit a plateau, begun its decline, and degenerated into a cesspool of ugly bigotry, gossip, slander, and legalism (Acts 21:20).

What went wrong? F. F. Bruce has taken this question on.[2] He identifies four dangers to which the Jerusalem church succumbed, and of which we should all be aware: cultural uniformity, a "safety first" mentality, legalism, and exclusivism. It is hard to argue with Bruce's points, and as I share my own observations, you will see that on many points he and I agree. One could argue that the Jerusalem church centralized and established a hierarchical leadership chain very quickly (Acts 6:1–6). The church had too many leaders, if we count the twelve apostles, who added seven more leaders; and then we find the elders leading under James's influence (some think the Jerusalem church had seventy elders). Add all this up, and you have almost ninety leaders. How could anything get done? The Jerusalem church also welcomed new "converts" from among the priests (Acts 6:7), which of course is not a bad thing. But something else occurred—the church allowed itself to be saturated and choked by a Judaic legalism (Acts 21:20).

The lack of true acceptance of other ethnic groups, even among those who had converted to Judaism, indicates a problem that eventually overcame the entire church. As Acts progresses, we see that it took great oration and persuasion on the part of Peter and James to prevent legalism from killing the entire new movement that was being born among the Gentiles (Acts 15:1–35). By the time we reach the end of Acts, we see that the church was so corrupted by legalism that many of its members even desired to have Paul, the writer of almost half the New Testament, imprisoned or killed. Paul was forced to compromise what he had learned and fought for, but he was still mobbed and arrested. Even in jail he was targeted for death (Acts 23:12–22). Granted, one cannot say that the church was responsible for all of this; Luke attributes these deeds to "the Jews," but by this time the Jerusalem church had become mainstream and was really viewed as just another conservative sect of Judaism. I am not discounting that there were true believers in the Jerusalem church, such as James; but the elders warned Paul of this very sort of reaction from those believers who had been among "the Jews" (Acts 21:20). The most alarming thing is that there is some indication that Paul was actually delivering a care package to the church from some Gentile churches abroad (Romans 15:25–27). The Jerusalem church accepted the money, but not the messenger. This was not a healthy church, nor is it a great example to us. In a matter of only forty years (that is, by 70 A.D.) the Jerusalem church was dead and gone forever.

I personally do not believe that the demise of the Jerusalem church was due strictly to structural issues or hierarchical development. The issue is much more basic. It is a matter of that church's DNA. The church was not obedient to the Head. It is as simple as that. In the very beginning, Jesus laid out strongly and clearly that His plan was for the church to receive an explosive power within that would spread out to the ends of the earth. He said (Acts 1:8), "You will receive power when the Holy Spirit has come upon you; and you shall be My witnesses both in Jerusalem, and in all Judea and Samaria, and even to the remotest part of the earth."

The Jerusalem church and especially the apostles were given very clear instructions. God held up His end by providing the power, but the disciples never left Jerusalem. In Acts 8:1 we read this: "On that day a great persecution began against the church in Jerusalem, and they were all scattered throughout the regions of Judea and Samaria, except the apostles."

After a short time of great blessings in Jerusalem, but without any mission beyond those borders, God had to force the early church out. In what may be the most ironic passage in the Bible, everyone is said to have spread out in Judea and Samaria *except the sent ones* (the apostles). Because our translations do not translate *apostolos* but simply use the transliteration of "apostle," and because we have come to think of the word *apostle* as a formal title, we tend to miss the obvious humor, even sarcasm, found in that verse. But it is there. Any first-century reader of the original language would have picked it up immediately.

In the original plan, the apostles were to go to Jerusalem, Judea, Samaria, and the outermost parts of the earth. Only persecution moved the people to reach Judea, which was a broader region but culturally and ethnically the same. To go to Samaria, however, was to cross a distinct cultural boundary in the eyes of the first-century Jews. The original plan that Jesus presented was clear, but it was quickly, even conveniently, forgotten by the apostles.

When the Gospel finally broke out among the Samaritans, the apostles had to be called in to sanction this new venture (Acts 8:4–24). It is interesting that the Gospel got there before the "sent ones," but it seems as if the Lord was waiting for them to catch up because the Holy Spirit did not fall on the new believers until Peter and John prayed for them. It feels as if the Lord was slowly egging on the "sent ones" to do what He had told them to. But they just didn't seem to understand.

God had to overtly interrupt Peter's meal plans with three incredible visions even to get him to be open to the idea of allowing "the way" to spread to the Gentiles. Nevertheless, for most of his life Peter was a little hesitant and incapable of committing himself to the mission among the Gentiles, preferring to be "the apostle to the Jews" (Galatians 2:7). Once Paul even sharply rebuked Peter in public for compromising his own convictions (Galatians 2:11–21). Again, it appears that God was pushing the "sent ones," and not in such subtle ways, but still they resisted.

God gave the apostles the opportunity to take the lead in a rapid movement that would ultimately spread around the world and even do what no nation had been able to do in a thousand years—overcome the great Roman Empire. And to carry this plan out, God used accidental church plants, ordinary nameless heroes, and the radical conversion of a violent Pharisee into an apostle who would reach the Gentiles.

The transition of leadership in the Jerusalem church provides us with a useful example. It began with eleven apostles to whom one more was added (Acts 1:16–26). Seven more were added (Acts 6:1–7), and the church was expanding quickly in Jerusalem because all the leaders were focused on winning others to Christ. As time passed, another leadership team (the elders) emerged, this one led by James. By the time we get to Acts 15, we find the elders on an equal footing with the apostles, and perhaps they even have an edge in the decision-making process. In Acts 21, only the elders remain.

In the Jerusalem church, as is often the case at the beginning of a church's life, the leaders were out ahead, showing the way and focusing on outreach. As time passed, the church became more internally focused. Those who still had a heart for outreach got marginalized and eventually found that serving outside the boundaries of the local church was more desirable. The church was left with more managerial leaders, who were devoted to internal care issues, and all outreach came to an end. And the very same pattern has been repeated throughout church history because we have never learned from the Jerusalem church's example.

We know that eventually the twelve apostles (minus James, who was martyred while still in Jerusalem) took to going out to the world, but it took far too long for the "sent ones" to actually get going. Others had to lead the way first.

Bigotry against the Gentiles, which was all too common in the Jewish establishment of the first century, eventually became the terminal disease that destroyed the Jerusalem church. At first the people in the Jerusalem church couldn't get along with Jews from other regions, or with new Jewish converts, and so separate ministries were formed with separate leaders (Acts 6:1–6). This was a move to accommodate rather than correct unhealthy spiritual practices. When we add to this mix a band of leaders who were content to stay in one place and serve just one kind of people, to the neglect of their Master's command, and who then compound that neglect with a large influx of religiously zealous priests, we end up with a church that has codified beliefs that substantiate her leaders' own prejudices.

The Antiochan church was far healthier than the Jerusalem church, and it accomplished a great deal more world-changing work, though at one point even this church suffered from the contagious bigotry of the Jerusalem church (Galatians 2:11–13). But as Acts progresses, I believe that we see the Holy Spirit being given the opportunity to continue teaching the apostles (in the person of Paul) to start and empower grassroots churches in more effective ways. In the New Testament, the model church that gets the greatest amount of scriptural attention—and the one, as a result, about which we can learn the most—is the Ephesian church. Perhaps we need to be learning more from some of these later and more advanced examples, and less from the one church that the book of Acts presents as so obviously unhealthy.

Notes

Preface and Acknowledgments

1. See Roland Allen, *Missionary Methods: St. Paul's or Ours* (London: World Dominion Press, 1953).
2. See J. Robert Clinton, *The Making of a Leader: Recognizing the Lessons and Stages of Leadership Development* (Colorado Springs, Colo.: IVP, 1988).
3. At the time he wrote *The Making of a Leader,* Dr. Clinton had studied seven hundred lives, but since then he has studied several hundred more.

Introduction: Life Is a Series of Adventurous Journeys

1. See Neil Cole and Robert E. Logan, *Raising Leaders for the Harvest* (Saint Charles, Ill.: Churchsmart Resources, 1995); Neil Cole, *TruthQuest: The Search for Spiritual Understanding* (Signal Hill, Calif.: CMA Resources, 2004); Neil Cole, *Organic Leadership: Leading Naturally Right Where You Are* (Grand Rapids, Mich.: Baker Books, 2009).
2. See Cole, *Organic Leadership*; Neil Cole, *Organic Church: Growing Faith Where Life Happens* (San Francisco: Jossey-Bass, 2005). See also Neil Cole, *Search & Rescue: Becoming a Disciple Who Makes a Difference* (Grand Rapids, Mich.: Baker Books, 2008), which looks at the apostle Paul and his philosophy of disciple-making, as deduced from the second epistle he wrote to Timothy.
3. See Eckhard Schnabel, *Paul the Missionary: Realities, Strategies and Methods* (Downers Grove, Ill.: IVP, 2008), and Eckhard Schnabel, *Early Christian Mission,* vols. 1 and 2 (Downers Grove, Ill.: IVP, 2004); the latter work will likely become a standard bearer and a source for works to follow. See also F. F. Bruce, *Commentary on the Book of the Acts: The English Text, with Introduction, Exposition, and Notes* (Grand Rapids, Mich.: Eerdmans, 1954), F. F. Bruce, *Paul: Apostle of the Heart Set Free* Grand Rapids, Mich.: Eerdmans, 2000), and John Pollock, *The Apostle: A Life of Paul* (Colorado Springs, Colo.: Victor Books, 1985).

Chapter 1: Born to a Destiny

1. Later Paul said of himself, "I was advancing in Judaism beyond many of my contemporaries among my countrymen, being more extremely zealous for my ancestral traditions" (Galatians 1:14).

2. Today it is common for tent makers to use the valued wool of black sheep from the region around Tarsus, and it may have been common then as well, although we do not know for sure.

3. We have no historical documentation to determine how long Paul remained in Tarsus, but his exceptional use of Greek is a strong indication that he was there at least through his formative early years. In his writings he seems to favor the Greek translation of the Old Testament, and so it is possible that Greek was his native tongue at home.

4. These trips would have been expensive even from as short a distance as Tarsus, but Saul's parents, because of their citizenship privileges, may have been able to afford such a trip once or twice.

5. Paul was a rising star in Judaism (see n. 1 above), but the Sanhedrin was made up mostly of powerful priestly families from the Jerusalem aristocracy, and so it would have been quite exceptional, and very unlikely, for Paul to have broken into that ruling council.

6. Peter Cole can be seen in many older and current documentary films about big-wave surfing, including *Step into Liquid, Riding Giants,* and *Surfing for Life.*

Chapter 2: New Life

1. As Luke does, I will use his Hebrew name, Saul, until we reach the point where Saul chooses to use his Latin name, Paul. It is likely that he had both names throughout his life and simply chose to use his Latin name when he was immersed in a culture where doing so would offer better opportunities and greater acceptance.

2. I admit that there are few who would read Luke's Acts the way I do. It certainly is a minority view to see Luke as being sarcastic about the fact that Peter and the other eleven disciples did not go out on mission in obedience to Jesus' command in Acts 1:8. Most see Luke as respectful throughout Acts, and as communicating a common purpose between Paul and Peter, and I too think this is true. But there is also another message to be found in the story. Luke is very precise in his language, and he commonly omits large amounts of information if it doesn't contribute to his message. If one compares the first half of Acts, which focuses on Peter, with the second half, which focuses on Paul, one sees a strong parallel. The reader sees Peter and Paul engaged in very similar or even the same acts—raising a paraplegic, pronouncing judgment on a Jewish magician, raising the dead, making a thrilling night-time escape from persecution, receiving visions and messages from the Lord, giving bold sermons in the face of persecutors. Peter's shadow heals; Paul's handkerchief heals. I believe that the message here is that Paul's apostolic authority is equal to Peter's. Therefore, if this message is one purpose of the writing, then there certainly is merit in reading Acts 8:1 as I do. Of course, Luke does portray the Jerusalem church as steadily declining in health over the course of the story, and it does not end well.

3. Saul's conversion has been pivotal in history as well: an enemy of the Way becomes its greatest proponent and establishes the church among the Gentiles. Throughout history, many others who attempted to refute the resurrection of Christ and the subsequent conversion of Saul also became proponents of the faith they once tried to disprove. Among them are the law professor Simon Greenleaf and the Oxford scholar and author C. S. Lewis. The latter, like Paul, paradoxically describes his youthful years as a time when he was a hostile atheist "angry with God for not existing"; see C. S. Lewis, *Surprised by Joy: The Shape of My Early Life* (New York: Harcourt, 1956), 115. Paul's testimony still stands as persuasive proof of the resurrection of Jesus. As Lyttleton once remarked, "The conversion and apostleship of St. Paul alone, duly considered, was of itself a demonstration sufficient to prove Christianity to be a divine revelation"; see George, Lord Lyttleton, *Observations on the Conversion and Apostleship of St. Paul: In a Letter to Gilbert West, Esq.* (London, 1747). Lyttleton's entire book is digitized and available for free: http://books.google.com/books?id=M54CAAAAQAAJ& printsec=frontcover&dq=G.+Lyttleton+The+conversion+and+apostle ship+of+St.+Paul&hl=en&ei=whRnTIHQCZ3YtAOdmqjqCg&sa=X& oi=book_result&ct=result&resnum=1&ved=0CCoQ6AEwAA#v=one page&q&f=false

4. That Paul saw the Lord is verified by the accounts of Ananias (Acts 9: 17) and Barnabas (Acts 9:27). It is probable that Saul's companions heard a loud noise but could not discern the words, much as the crowd heard a loud but indiscernible sound when the Father spoke to Jesus (John 12:29). According to the New American Standard Bible, Saul's companions could "not understand the voice of the One who was speaking" (Acts 22:9). Whatever they heard, the light, the noise, the reaction of Saul, and his resulting blindness must have been enough to cause them to take this event seriously and help Saul find a safe place to make sense of it.

5. In his outstanding commentary, F .F. Bruce poses a question and leaves it hanging: Did Jesus speak in Aramaic because it was His mother tongue or because it was Saul's? It is likely that Saul's first language was Greek. Perhaps Jesus spoke in Aramaic because He was addressing a Pharisee of the strictest order. Many Israeli Messianic scholars believe that Paul, who describes himself as having been "a Hebrew of the Hebrews," was an expert in letters and fluent in Hebrew, and so it may be that this was simply the risen Lord speaking in His own familiar tongue. See F. F. Bruce, *The Book of the Acts*, rev. ed. (Grand Rapids, Mich.: Eerdmans, 1988), 182*n*14.

6. Ananias, a disciple living in Damascus, was a devout Jew (Acts 22:12). He received a vision from the Lord, Who told him to go to Saul, heal him, and give him his new calling. Ananias was somewhat hesitant, having heard of Saul and his notorious reputation, and so the Lord told him the details of Saul's conversion and new calling. The Lord also confirmed that Saul would experience suffering himself: "Go," he said to Ananias, "for he is a

chosen instrument of Mine, to bear My name before the Gentiles and kings and the sons of Israel; for I will show him how much he must suffer for My name's sake."

7. See John Pollock, *The Apostle: A Life of Paul* (Colorado Springs, Colo.: Victor Books, 1985), 53.

8. It is said in Deuteronomy 25:2–3 that the maximum permissible number of lashes is forty, probably because more would be lethal. The Jews, always aware of the lines drawn by Mosaic law, would have wished to reduce the number of lashes to thirty-nine: the Mishnah (Makkoth 3:10) prescribes the punishment as thirty-nine lashes to keep the punishers from overstepping the legal limit (if only through some accident of counting), and thirty-eight lashes would have been thought too few.

9. See Ralph Martin, *Word Biblical Commentary: 2 Corinthians* (Waco, Tex.: Word Books, 1986), 376–77.

10. See Makkoth 3.2.11. The Talmud was not written down until much later than the New Testament, and so we cannot be entirely confident that the practices mentioned in the written Talmud were carried out during the first century exactly as prescribed there. Thus there are grounds for speculation, and of course some men may have acted unjustly in ways that suited their own agendas, as we see occurring a few times in the New Testament.

11. Pollock, *The Apostle*, 53–54.

12. It is generally agreed that 2 Corinthians (56 A.D.), where Paul mentions three shipwrecks (2 Corinthians 11:25), was written before Paul's shipwreck on his way to Rome, mentioned in Acts; therefore, Paul experienced at least four shipwrecks.

13. By this time, however, Stephen had been killed, and Philip had settled in Caesarea, and so "the Seven," as they were called, were by now probably not as prominent in Jerusalem, after the persecution that Saul had led.

14. Many place this visit, mentioned in Galatians 2:1 ff., during the trip described in Acts 15, and this is also a viable explanation.

15. One could argue that this band was missing a female perspective. Leadership in later churches would have this important point of view as well (Acts 16:14–15, 17:4; Romans 16:1–16).

16. See Neil Cole, *Church 3.0: Upgrades for the Future of the Church* (San Francisco: Jossey-Bass, 2010), where I expound on the reasons why a leadership team of five is best.

17. J. Robert Clinton, *The Making of a Leader: Recognizing the Lessons and Stages of Leadership Development* (Colorado Springs, Colo.: IVP, 1988), 238.

Chapter 3: The First Journey

1. There had been an Ethiopian missionary who was sent back to his homeland to take the Gospel there, and others had gone to parts of Samaria and Judea.

Even Paul had visited Arabia. But this was the first time a local church, led by the Spirit, had sent a missionary team for the purpose of making disciples of people overseas, an expedition that would result in the starting of indigenous churches, which in turn would start others.

2. See John Pollock, *The Apostle: A Life of Paul* (Colorado Springs, Colo.: Victor Books, 1985), 71.

3. There are a few inscriptions found on Cyprus that may or may not refer to Sergius Paulus. Sir William Ramsay found an inscription in 1912 that he thought supported the claim that some of the family members of Sergius Paulus, including one of his daughters, became Christians because of his witness.

4. Eckhard Schnabel, *Paul the Missionary: Realities, Strategies and Methods* (Downers Grove, Ill.: IVP, 2008), 79.

5. As an example of such usage in the book of Acts, Cornelius is told to bring his household (*oikos*) together to hear a message from Peter (Acts 11: 13–14). When Peter arrives, Cornelius is expecting him and has gathered his relatives and close friends (Acts 10:24), a group made up of more than just his immediate family and including the people socially connected to him. We are told that the message was heard by a large gathering of people (Acts 11:13–14). Luke consistently demonstrates that the *oikos* was a primary means of spreading the message—with Lydia (Acts 16:15), the Philippian jailer (Acts 16:31), and Crispus (Acts 18:18).

6. See also Neil Cole, *Organic Church: Growing Faith Where Life Happens* (San Francisco: Jossey-Bass, 2005).

7. Eckhard Schnabel, *Early Christian Mission,* vol. 2 (Downers Grove, Ill.: IVP, 2004), 1084–88.

8. As noted earlier, Luke refers to the missionary band at one point (Acts 13:13) as "Paul and his companions," which may reflect a bias that could have offended John Mark.

9. In any case, most scholars believe that the Gospel of Mark was written later. Early tradition sets the writing shortly after Peter's death, around 65 A.D.

10. In the Acts narrative, Luke considers Antioch of Asia to be in Pisidia rather than Galatia, but the city was not actually in Pisidia. Rome considered it part of Galatia, although geographically it was in Phrygia. Borders shifted frequently at that time, and what had been established politically did not always match people's cultural perceptions. It seems that the people of that region did not consider the city to be in Galatia, since it was not part of that historic or ethnic region, which is further north. It was close enough to Pisidia, however, that it was called Pisidian Antioch, as a way to distinguish it from the other Antiochs in the world, all named after Antiochus. At any rate, the churches in this region are the ones to which Paul wrote the Galatian letter.

11. Commonly in Acts, Luke first summarizes what took place and then provides the details.

12. Some contend that the name *Je-sus* or *Iesous* was used because it sounds like "Hail, Zeus" or another translation of "Jupiter Zeus." A good book to read on how the Greeks thought of Christianity and applied the Zeus typology to Jesus is Richard Tarnas, *The Passion of the Western Mind* (New York: Ballantine, 1991).

13. There is much debate about the chronology of Paul's three visits to Jerusalem and about his accounts mentioned in the Galatian epistle. I favor the view that if Paul had written the letter after his visit to Jerusalem, he would have mentioned the letter drafted by James regarding the subject, thus settling things once and for all. This is especially true, given the portions of Galatians that specifically address his visits to Jerusalem and his interactions with the church's leadership. It seems unrealistic that he would have left that information out of this letter, in view of the letter's subject matter and overall purpose, if it had been written later. There are strong views on both sides of the issue, of course. I have chosen this chronology but share it here not in definitive language but in the language of probability.

14. F. F. Bruce, *The Book of the Acts,* rev. ed. (Grand Rapids, Mich.: Eerdmans, 1988), 282.

Chapter 4: The Second Journey

1. Acts of Paul and Thecla 3.3. See also William M. Ramsay, *The Church in the Roman Empire Before A.D. 170* (Boston: Longwood Press, 1978), 31–32.

2. Many place the writing of the Galatian letter later than this. I think that if the Jerusalem council had met before the letter was written, that would have carried some weight in the letter, but the meeting of the Jerusalem council goes unmentioned in the letter to the Galatians.

3. Of course the original missionary band included John Mark, but only while the missionaries were on Cyprus. The vast majority of the work in the Galatian region was done by Paul and Barnabas alone, and so this new team is double in size. As for Luke's involvement, he does not mention his own name. He simply uses the first-person plural in recounting those portions of the narrative in which he is a member of the group. This change in pronouns occurs twice in Acts and is Luke's subtle and humble way of revealing his involvement.

4. This region to the north (along with Asia Minor, to the south) is today in Turkey. At the top of this region is the modern-day city of Istanbul, a place where East and West meet and are separated by a strategic water passage. Later in history, this place would come to be of great significance to Christendom as the capital of Christianity, known as Constantinople.

5. Again (see note 3 to this chapter), Luke's involvement can be discerned from his use of the first-person plural.

6. Paul, writing to this church later on, would appeal to the members' sense of pride in their citizenship by reminding them that their citizenship was now in heaven (Philippians 3:20–21).

7. William M. Ramsay, *St. Paul: The Traveler and Roman Citizen,* rev. ed. (Grand Rapids, Mich.: Kregel, 2001), 174.

8. Granted, this is a puzzle, and I am trying to put the pieces together in a manner that makes sense. I believe that this is as good an explanation for these events as any and actually fits the pieces together best.

9. It is significant that Paul received a specific vision of the man. The man was clearly Macedonian, and Paul could see his entire body ("he was standing"). It may be that his accent revealed him to be Macedonian, but Luke's description of the vision seems to indicate that he recognized him as Macedonian from his appearance. Maybe Paul was literally able to read the inscriptions on the jailer's uniform. One possible scenario is that Paul, upon seeing this man at the site of the beating, knew that he had to hold his tongue and get through the beating in order to gain access to this Macedonian man and help him and his household.

10. Although Luke's summation seems to indicate that Timothy stayed with Silas in Berea, other New Testament documents clarify that Timothy was in fact left in Thessalonica (1 Thessalonians 3:1–6). It is possible that Paul sent Timothy back to Thessalonica from Berea, since he himself went on to Athens, leaving Silas in Berea. This possibility does not in any way change my proposition regarding Paul's shift in strategy from the first journey.

11. Geoffrey W. Bromiley et al. (eds.), *The International Standard Bible Encyclopedia,* vol. 1 (Grand Rapids, Mich.: Eerdmans, 1978), 287–88.

12. At this point, navigating Acts is a challenge. Luke interrupts the chronological flow with parenthetical summations and then gets back into the chronological flow to relay some of the details. He does something similar on the first journey, when he summarizes how Paul and Barnabas went from town to town preaching (Acts 14:6–7) and then jumps back into describing the details of what happened (Acts 14:8 ff.). As a result, I find it illogical to follow the chapter verse by verse in strictly chronological fashion, although it is progressive. I believe that Luke, in describing Paul's Corinthian experience, first gives a general summation, telling how the events there took place and how the work started (Acts 18:1–8), and then, in a parenthetical thought, gets specific about two things— what occurred to get the work started, and how long it would last (Acts 18:9–11). The narration then goes into more detail about how the work arrived at its end (Acts 18:12–18). It would make no sense for Jesus to tell Paul to "not be silent" in the midst of very fruitful advances well into a rapidly expanding movement. The next statement, "And he settled there a year and six months," indicates an overall parenthetical summation tied specifically to the previous thought regarding Paul's nighttime vision of Jesus. In other words, Paul saw Jesus, and as a result he stayed in Corinth for a year and six months, which is how all of this happened. Luke then dives back into specifics, to show us what gets us to the end. As we will see, another parenthetical paragraph slipped in at the end of this chapter

(Acts 18:24–28) is equally hard to place precisely in its chronology, but I hope in this book to clarify the placement of that paragraph.

13. The Isthmian games, much like the Olympiad, were held for centuries in the years before and after the Olympic games, and always in Corinth. A winner received a wreath of celery or woven pine needles, which Paul alludes to in writing to the Corinthians (1 Corinthians 9:25).

14. Many commentators assume that Priscilla and Aquila were already believers, but that is not necessarily true. There is really no evidence of Christians in Rome at this point. Luke mentions the fact that they were Jews, not Christians. We have already seen (Acts 17:33–34) that Luke does not always mention the baptism of new converts when they believed. I think that Luke is describing Paul living out the new insights he has received from Jesus, and that these are the first of many people He will have in this city. Luke tells us that Aquila and Priscilla have come to Corinth because they were exiled from Rome by the emperor's edict banishing Jews. Many believe that they were exiled from Rome because of their faith in Christ, after Claudius's imperial edict in 49–50 A.D. The edict, commonly referred to as the one identified by Suetonius in his *Life of Claudius* (24.4), refers to "Jews [who] were indulging in constant riots at the instigation of Chrestus, [whom] he banished from Rome" ("Chrestus" is assumed to be a reference to Christ). The thought is that the Romans would have supposed Him to be a Jewish rebel stirring up riots between the traditional Jews and the new sect. There is certainly some merit to this proposition, which makes it likely that Aquila and Priscilla became Christians before meeting Paul, but Luke does not state as much. Luke tells us plainly that they were banished from Rome because they were "Jews" (Acts 18:2). Given Luke's obvious bias, it does seem unlikely that he would say they were exiled because they were "Jews" if indeed it was for their faith in Christ. The description found in the edict certainly does not reflect either our Lord or His followers, but when did the edicts of secular governments ever reflect the righteousness of God or His people? Whether Aquila and Priscilla were Christians before or after they met Paul, he certainly influenced them, and a lifelong partnership in spreading the Gospel was begun.

15. Erastus's name is actually inscribed on a sidewalk stone in the amphitheater at Corinth, and you can see it to this day. Paul is only one of many believers through the centuries to have left a mark on Corinth.

16. The Western text, which the King James Version leans on for translation, also mentions that Paul was in a hurry to get back to Jerusalem for the Passover feast, and so he may have been trying to catch a boat as well.

17. Luke simply says, "And having spent some time there, he left."

18. Luke does mention that Apollos was learned in the Scriptures and had an understanding of Jesus but was only familiar with John's baptism. This could mean that he was unfamiliar with the doctrine of Christian baptism, but one can argue from the book of Acts that baptism is tied directly to an

understanding of the Gospel and salvation. Aquila and Priscilla certainly recognized Apollos's profound giftedness and passion, but also his incorrect understanding. They explained more of who Christ is and what He had done. It is plausible that Apollos knew about Christ before meeting these two and simply misunderstood a nonessential doctrine, for there was a church in his hometown of Alexandria. But Luke makes it clear that Apollos had limited knowledge of Christ, and that he was influenced by the teaching of John the Baptist. For Luke to make mention of the correction suggests that it was more than just a few blanks with respect to nonessential doctrines. Perhaps Apollos was acquainted with Jesus as Messiah and even as a substitutionary atonement, as John was (John 1:29), but did not yet know of the death, burial, or resurrection. If so, then his message would have been that of repentance and righteousness—perhaps even of following Christ— but without the Gospel, his ministry would have lacked power for salvation (Romans 1:16). This would certainly best fit the description presented by Luke. It is not by coincidence that Luke goes on, in the very next paragraph, to describe in some detail other disciples of John the Baptist, showing that they had not understood the Gospel or received the Holy Spirit. It is not unreasonable that Apollos was in the same place—a disciple mighty in Scripture, knowing about Jesus but not yet about the death, burial, and resurrection, and therefore not yet regenerate and full of the Holy Spirit. Regardless, Apollos was deficient in his understanding of the work of Christ and was quite responsive to the tutelage of Aquila and Priscilla, who are mentored by Paul. The results still come out to be an astonishing reproduction of Paul's ministry practice, passed on through three generations.

19. Luke has a habit of filling his parchment. His Gospel and Acts are the longest books of the New Testament in terms of length (not the number of chapters but the number of words), and together they amount to about half of the New Testament. Some scholars believe that for both volumes, he wrote until he reached the end of the parchment.

20. Even if you choose not to accept my interpretations of this passage, the outcomes are still valid, as are the overall observations of Paul's experiences and the lessons he learned. He still changed his strategy on the basis of Jesus' words. He still found workers in the city, and they began to multiply, beginning with Priscilla and Aquila and then going on to Apollos and beyond. From this point on, Paul's strategy was no longer that of an itinerant. He stayed in one place longer, raised disciples from the harvest, trained them on the job, and sent them out as self-sufficient missionaries.

21. After the conversation, I took it out of the trash and put it on my reading pile. I had just wanted to make a point to Brad, and he got it. I confess, though, that I never did get around to reading the proposal. Brad has since planted many churches and also founded Kingdom Causes, which is expanding into multiple cities and municipalities, bringing kingdom transformation where it is so badly needed today: http://kingdomcauses.org.

22. See. for example, the fairly recent U.S. editions of two classics by the British author C. S. Lewis, *The Problem of Pain* (San Francisco: HarperSanFrancisco, 2001) and *A Grief Observed* (San Francisco: HarperSanFrancisco, 2001). See also Philip Yancey, *Where Is God When It Hurts?* (Grand Rapids, Mich.: Zondervan, 1977).

Chapter 5: The Third Journey

1. J. Robert Clinton, *The Making of a Leader: Recognizing the Lessons and Stages of Leadership Development* (Colorado Springs, Colo.: IVP, 1988), 46.

2. Kirsopp Lake and Henry Joel Cadbury (eds.), *The Beginnings of Christianity,* part 1: *The Acts of the Apostles,* vol. 4: *English Translation and Commentary* (London: Macmillan, 1933), 239.

3. These two-plus years, combined with the three months spent working out of the synagogue, came to about three years in total (Acts 20:31); see F. F. Bruce, *The Book of the Acts,* rev. ed. (Grand Rapids, Mich.: Eerdmans, 1988), 366.

4. It is entirely possible that Pergamum won the competition for spiritual influence, since Jesus refers to Pergamum as the place where Satan dwells.

5. William Barclay, *The New Daily Study Bible: The Acts of the Apostles* (Louisville: John Knox Press, 1975), 164–65.

6. Ibid., 164.

7. Some are not surprised to discover that just before World War II, Adolf Hitler relocated this altar to Berlin, where it remains to this day in the Pergamum Museum. The altar is considered the "throne of Satan," and Hitler was in search of occult artifacts that he thought could grant him power.

8. Bruce, *The Book of the Acts,* 368.

9. It is probably no coincidence that the same loathing of Jews was also evident among the Nazis, and so perhaps Satan's throne room is full of hatred for God's chosen people.

10. In museums even today there are many samples of these sorts of magical papyri. Bruce, *The Book of the Acts,* 369, cites London, Paris, and Leiden as the places where the most voluminous collections of such papyri are found. Princeton University also has a sample, translated and expounded upon by the Greek scholar B. M. Metzger, "St. Paul and the Magicians," *Princeton Seminary Bulletin* 38 (1944), 27–30.

11. It is interesting that the word used to describe this riotous mob is *ekklesia,* which is the word our Bible translates as "church." This group of highly energized, angry people shouting their allegiance to a false god may be the largest "church" gathering mentioned in the New Testament. I think I've been to that church before!

12. It is not popular to think of Titus as having deserted Paul for love of the world. It is clear that Demas has done so (2 Timothy 4:10), but the reality is that Titus and Crescens are included in Paul's words about desertion.

For one thing, only one verb is used for all three. Moreover, there are many places where the letter could have mentioned Titus and Crescens and put them in a favorable light, as Paul had done with others, but he chose to limit his mention of them to a single sentence and a single verb. Exegetically speaking, it is irresponsible to make excuses for Titus when Paul himself did not. This is probably the best explanation for why Luke never mentions any of the people just named.

13. This may seem like a semantic argument, especially given Paul's instructions to Titus to appoint elders (Titus 1:5), but I do believe that the concept of raising leaders who are less dependent, and who are sufficient in the Holy Spirit, is indeed a profound lesson that he had learned since his first missionary journey, and one that bore significant fruit this time around.

14. Today we have the second and third letters that he wrote, now labeled the first and the second, respectively, but the first one is lost (1 Corinthians 5:9).

Chapter 6: The Fourth Journey

1. Many consider this a reference to his standing before Caesar during his second and last Roman imprisonment, when he wrote the epistle to Timothy. I personally believe that this is a reference to his first trial before Caesar, which occurred during his fourth journey, because he was delivered during that defense, not during his last one.

2. I have intentionally written these questions from our point of view, and in the language of our own context. I am certain that the Jews in Paul's day would have couched these issues in entirely different language.

3. In Acts 10:27–29, Peter tells Cornelius that it is unlawful for him as a Jew to enter a Gentile home. But this was from oral law, not Mosaic Law, which indicates some confusion. This is what also led him, in Antioch, to separate from the Gentiles at meals (Galatians 2:11–21).

4. Of course, when we read Galatians and Romans, which were likely written at this time, it is easy for us to see how this rumor may have gained momentum. Paul's view of the law and the Jerusalem church's view of the law were probably very different by this time.

5. See http://julianspriggs.com/annascaiaphas.aspx

6. Flavius Josephus, *Antiquities of the Jews* 20:198.

7. Today there are no venomous snakes on Malta, but apparently there were during the first century, and the natives of the island were well acquainted with them.

8. From a portion of the letter from Ignatius to the Ephesian church.

Conclusion: The Final Journey

1. Eckhard Schnabel, *Paul the Missionary: Realities, Strategies and Methods* (Downers Grove, Ill.: IVP, 2008), 116.

2. See note 12 to chapter 5.

3. The information about miles traveled by Paul is from Schnabel, *Paul the Missionary*, 122. For the shipwrecks, see note 12 to Chapter Two. With respect to churches that Paul started in his lifetime, some have said that there were only fourteen, but I would assume that a number of other churches were also started but not necessarily named as churches. For instance, there is no mention of a church started in Athens, but there were households there that began to follow Christ, and so we can assume that a church was born there. In Philippi, there were two households that surrendered to the Gospel, and so there could have been two organic churches there. Some say that there was just one church in Philippi, because Paul wrote a letter to its members, but the letter is actually to the saints in Christ who were in Philippi. Thus it's a challenge to number the churches that Paul started. We have already noted that he started only the Ephesian church in Asia, which in turn started many others. There are also places where no churches are said to have been started, but we do know that Paul was preaching in such places (for example, in Illyricum). Did Paul start churches while he was in Damascus? Someone did, but it probably wasn't Paul, since he was on his way to Damascus to arrest Christians. But when he went to Arabia he may have started churches. Some assume he was just on retreat, listening to the Lord, but he was driven away by the police, so we can assume that he did some preaching. Did he start churches while he was in Tarsus? Acts does mention churches in Syria (Acts 15:40–41). Could it be that some of them were started before he was sent from Antioch? And did Paul go to Spain? If so, then perhaps he started churches there as well, but we do not know. At any rate, he probably started close to twenty churches himself, with many more born from those. Finally, regarding the two letters written by Paul that are not in the New Testament, his actual first letter to the Corinthians is mentioned in the letter that we now call 1 Corinthians (1 Corinthians 5:9), and his letter to the Laodiceans is also mentioned in that letter (Corinthians 4:16).

4. This prison is called Peter's prison, too, because Peter may have been there just before his own execution, although he did not write his epistles from there.

5. See Neil Cole, *Organic Leadership: Leading Naturally Right Where You Are* (Grand Rapids, Mich.: Baker Books, 2009), 154–55, and J. Robert Clinton, *Clinton Leadership Commentary*, vol. 1 (Alta Dena, Calif.: Barnabas Publications, 1999). See also J. Robert Clinton, "Three Articles About Finishing Well," available free from his Web site: www.bobbyclinton.com/articles/downloads/3finishwellarticles.pdf.

6. Clinton, "Three Articles About Finishing Well."

7. Neil Cole, *Search & Rescue: Becoming a Disciple Who Makes a Difference* (Grand Rapids, Mich.: Baker Books, 2008), 142–43.

Appendix 2: What Went Wrong with the Jerusalem Church?

1. Much of what is presented in this appendix is adapted from Neil Cole, *Church 3.0: Upgrades for the Future of the Church* (San Francisco: Jossey-Bass, 2010).
2. See F. F. Bruce, "The Church of Jerusalem," *Christian Brethren Research Fellowship Journal* 4 (April 1964), 5–14.

The Author

Neil Cole is an experienced church planter and pastor as well as an international speaker. In addition to having founded the Awakening Chapels, which are reaching young postmodern people in urban settings, he is also a founder of Church Multiplication Associates (CMA), which has trained more than forty thousand people in organic church planting over the last ten years and has churches throughout the United States and in more than forty countries. Neil is also one of the key founding leaders of the simple church movement, which is rapidly growing around the world. Currently Neil serves as executive director of CMAResources. He is responsible for providing church leaders with the ministry tools needed to reproduce healthy disciples, leaders, churches, and movements. His responsibilities also include developing, training, and coaching church planters.

Neil Cole is the author of *Cultivating a Life for God: Multiplying Disciples Through Life Transformation Groups* (1999); *TruthQuest: The Search for Spiritual Understanding* (2004); *Organic Church: Growing Faith Where Life Happens* (2005); *Search & Rescue: Becoming a Disciple Who Makes a Difference* (2008); *Organic Leadership: Leading Naturally Right Where You Are* (2009); and *Church 3.0: Upgrades for the Future of the Church* (2010). He is coauthor (with Paul Kaak) of *Organic Church Planters' Greenhouse: The First Story* (2004) and (with Robert E. Logan) of *Raising Leaders for the Harvest* (1995) and *Beyond Church Planting: Pathways for Emerging Churches* (2005). He lives in Long Beach, California, with his wife, Dana, and their three children, Heather, Erin, and Zachary.

— Scripture Index —

— Subject Index —

Page numbers followed by *fig* indicate a photograph.

Publius, 123
The Purpose-Driven Church (Warren), 127, 128

Q

Quirinius, governor of Syria, 120

R

Radical salvation, 37–38
Ramsay, William, 72
Renewal, 139
Republic (Plato), 30
Revelation, book of, 130
Ridley, Charles, 81
Road to Damascus conversion, 19, 21, 23–24
Rohn, Jim, 113
Roman citizenship (*civis Romanus*), 7, 70–71, 119
Rome: Mamertine prison where Paul was held, 132*fig*, 135; Paul's imprisonment in, 113–114, 121–126, 128–131; second imprisonment and beheading of Paul in, 134–135; shipwrecked on the way to, 122–123
Rufus, 35
Ruiz, Rosie, 133

S

Sanhedrin (high court of Israel): Gamaliel's counsel to the, 9; Paul brought before the Jerusalem, 118–121; Paul as possible member of, 8; Saul's persecution agenda approved by, 22. *See also* Judaism
Saul, King, 6
Saul of Tarsus (later Paul): Ananias' healing and instruction of, 24, 25–26, 28, 39; Antioch church leadership by, 33–36; birth and early life of, 6–9; called to preach to the Gentiles, 29; church leadership formed by, 34–36; denounces Bar-Jesus, 49; development after return to Tarsus, 29–33; early mentors and Pharisee education of,

9; elects to use his Roman name of Paul, 50; family of, 6–7, 30; healed of his blindness, 24–25; on his past and looking forward, 12–13; imagining emotions of, 47, 48; isolation lessons experienced by, 42; languages spoken by, 7–8; Perge bathhouse site of preaching by, 45*fig*–46*fig*; persecution agenda approved by the Sanhedrin, 22; preaching the Gospel in the synagogues, 31–32; presence during Stephen's execution, 20, 22–23; remembrance of Stephen's words by, 38; Road to Damascus conversion of, 19, 21, 23–24; Roman citizenship of, 7, 70–71, 119; statement to the Mars Hill philosophers by, 47; whipped by the Jews, 30–31. *See also* Paul (formerly Saul of Tarsus)
Saul's early mission travels: to Antioch, 33, 34–35; the beginning of, 26–27; rejection in Arabia, Damascus, and Jerusalem, 27–29; return to Jerusalem, 33–34; return to Tarsus for 10 years, 29–33. *See also* Paul's first journey
Schnabel, Eckhard, 50, 51
School of Tyrannus, 99, 126
Search & Rescue (Cole), 14, 140
Second-journey leaders: learning from what works and what doesn't, 88–89; listening in season of aloneness and fear, 89–91; necessity of suffering, 86–89; practical ideas for second-journey leaders, 91
Sergii Paulii, 51
Sergius Paulus, 49, 50, 53
The Seven (Hellenistic Jewish leaders), 33
Silas: arrested with Paul in Philippi, 72–74; referred to as a prophet, 35; stays behind with the Berea church, 75; travels with Paul to visit first journey churches, 84–85
Simeon (called Niger), 35
Simon of Cyrene, 35